C000279976

THE SAINTS
by Luke Barnes

A NUFFIELD PRODUCTION

The Saints was first performed on 5 August 2014 as part of the Art at the Heart festival at Nuffield Playing Field in Guildhall Square, Southampton. Nuffield Playing Field was built by Assemble Architects. The festival was supported by The Sackler Foundation, Arts Council England and Southampton City Council.

Nuffield is supported by Arts Council England, Southampton City Council, Hampshire County Council and University of Southampton

Registered charity number: 286876

Please note this went to print during rehearsals
and so the script may differ slightly in the final production.

Nuffield is Southampton's leading professional theatre company based at the Nuffield Theatre at the heart of the Highfield campus of the University of Southampton. The Company is led by Sam Hodges, supported by a team of associates – directors Blanche McIntyre, Natalie Abrahami and Michael Longhurst, designer Tom Scutt and playwright Adam Brace – and develops and produces work with some of the UK's most exciting and dynamic theatre companies. In 2014 Nuffield appointed Samantha Bond, Laura Carmichael, Tom Hiddleston and Celia Imrie as Associate Actors.

Nuffield celebrated its 50th anniversary season in 2014/15. The season featured four new commissions and highlights included Hampshire Youth Theatre's stage adaptation of Michael Morpurgo's *The Best Christmas Present in the World*, adapted by Oliver Birch; the world premiere of the stage adaptation of the classic Coen Brothers' film *The Hudsucker Proxy* (7 – 30 May 2015) in a co-production with Liverpool Everyman & Playhouse; *The Snow Queen* (27 Nov 2014 – 4 Jan 2015) written by Georgia Pritchett (*The Thick of It*, *Veep*) and in partnership with Royal & Derngate, Northampton; the return of the critically acclaimed Nuffield production of Caryl Churchill's *A Number* with a transfer to the Young Vic in London; and Nuffield Youth Theatre's production of Philip Pullman's *His Dark Materials*, with both parts performed in repertory.

At the heart of Nuffield's mission is a commitment to artist development, with the launch of Nuffield Laboratory in 2014; a creative hub for developing new work and nurturing creative talent. The programme offers residencies, workshops, creative development and networking opportunities to local artists.

Nuffield Connect aims to enrich people's experience of Nuffield through a vibrant year round programme of engagement and enrichment. Nuffield Connect engages over 5,000 people through its programme animation activities, including its Youth Theatre and Drama Club and its adult workshops and outreach projects including RSC Open Stages. Nuffield also continues to host the prestigious Hampshire Youth Theatre annually.

Find out more about Nuffield at:
nuffieldtheatre.co.uk
🖤 **@nuffieldtheatre**

Nuffield Supporters 2014

We are very grateful for the generous support we receive from the following organisations and individuals, without whom our ambitious programme would not be able to happen:

Core Supporters:

Arts Council England, Southampton City Council, Hampshire County Council, University of Southampton

Corporate Supporters:

Covers Builders Merchants, Daily Echo, Draper Tools, Fiander Tovell LLP, Fonix, Hendy Van & Truck, Logic Mighty, Wave 105FM, Williams Shipping

Donations and Grants:

Barker Mill Foundation, The Ernest Cook Charitable Trust, The Esmée Fairbairn Foundation, The Foyle Foundation, The Sackler Foundation, The Wolfson Foundation

Nuffield Friends, Members and Producing Circle

Find out more about ways to support Nuffield at nuffieldtheatre.co.uk/support-us or call Victor Manley on 023 8031 550 ext 232

Be a Saint

We hope you enjoyed today's production of *The Saints*. Nuffield is a charity dedicated to creating new theatre for the City of Southampton. Box Office revenue and core funding only ever cover half of the production costs of putting on a show like *The Saints*. Please consider donating to our crowdfunding fundraising campaign. In return for your donation you'll have the opportunity to receive rewards such as limited edition memorabilia or VIP parties with Saints legends.

#beasaint
nuffieldtheatre.co.uk/support-us/be-a-saint

NUFFIELD STAFF

ARTISTIC AND PRODUCING
Creative and Executive Director
Sam Hodges
Associate Producer
Annie Reilly
Associate Directors
Natalie Abrahami
Michael Longhurst
Blanche McIntyre
Associate Designer
Tom Scutt
Associate Playwright
Adam Brace
Artist Development Producer
Dawn Taylor
Community Producer
Sharon Lawless
Youth Theatre Director
Max Lindsay
Youth Theatre Producer
Chris Duncan
Youth Theatre Apprentice
Ruby Carr

ADMINISTRATION
Administrative Director/Deputy CEO
James Gough
Office Administrator
Alison Thurley

COMMUNICATIONS AND DEVELOPMENT
Development and Communications Director
Alexandra Marshall
Development Officer
Victor Manley
Marketing Officer
Christiane Hofmann
Press Assistant
Chris Duncan
Membership Secretary
Michele Wilson
Box Office Manager
Annie Pearce
Box Office Assistants
Rebecca D'Silva
Vic Fabian
Justin Gamblin
Eileen Harding
Patricia McCoy
Elena Pearce
Liz Talbot
Faye Timby

CAST

KENNY	**Cary Crankson**
EMILY	**Scarlett Alice Johnson**
MUM	**Claire-Louise Cordwell**
JOEY	**Harry Hepple**
JEREMY MCCARDLE	**Carl Prekopp**
CARL	**Matthew Raymond**
JOHNNO	**Claire-Louise Cordwell**
COLIN	**Will Stokes**
DAVE JONES	**Tendayi Jembere**
COMMENTATOR 1	
COMMENTATOR 2	
GRANDSTAND VOICE	
GEORGINA	
SARAH-JANE	
DOCTOR	
MATT LE TISSIER	**Matt Le Tissier**
FRANCIS BENALI	**Francis Benali**
FANATIC	
CLOWN	
DAD	
VICAR	
TED BATES	
CHORUS	

All other parts played by the company.
Local community choirs perform as the chorus.

CREATIVE AND PRODUCTION TEAM

Matthew Dunster	Director
Luke Barnes	Writer
Anna Fleischle	Costume and Set Designer
Charlotte Broom	Choreographer
Joshua Carr	Lighting Designer
Emma Laxton	Sound Designer
Dick Straker	Video and Projection Designer
Anna Cooper	Casting Director
Richard Pinner	Magic Consultant
Tim Anger	Site Production Manager
Michael Ager	*The Saints* Production Manager
Neil Starke	Senior Technician
Graham Ward	Sound Technician
Joseph Kennion	Lighting Technician
Tom Robinson	Technician and Carpenter
Tom Holloway	Technician
Nikki Colclough	Company Stage Manager
Will Treasure	Deputy Stage Manager
Charlotte Dodson	Assistant Stage Manager
Aly Fielden	Wardrobe Mistress
Ilona Karas	Costume Supervisor

With special thanks to:

Assemble Architects, Francis Benali, Matt Le Tissier, Michael Thew, James Wilson, Paul Hingston, Fonix, Chris Williams at Willbox, Williams Shipping, Lisa Gowling, Saints Foundation, Southampton FC, Saints Foundation Choirs, Wildern Community Choir.

CAST BIOGRAPHIES

Claire-Louise Cordwell
Trained at the Royal Academy of Dramatic Art.
Theatre: *Carthage* (Finborough Theatre); *Dangerous Lady* (Theatre Royal, Stratford East); *Beautiful Thing* (Royal Exchange); *The Swan* (National Theatre); *There is a War* (National Theatre); *Ecstasy* (Hampstead and West End); *Oleanna* (York Theatre Royal); *Orphans* (Paines Plough); *The Frontline* (Globe); *Othello* (Frantic Assembly); *Torn* (Arcola); *Dirty Butterfly* (Young Vic); *Days of Significance* (Royal Shakespeare Company/Tricycle); *Burn/ Chatroom/ Citizenship* (National Theatre); *Stoning Mary* (Royal Court); *Compact Failure* (Clean Break)
Television: *Line of Duty* (BBC2); *The Honourable Woman* (BBC); *Holby City* (BBC); *Call the Midwife* (BBC); *Casualty* (BBC); *Doctors* (BBC); *The Bill* (ITV); *Law and Order* (ITV); *Day of the Triffids* (BBC); *EastEnders* (BBC); *Trial & Retribution* (ITV); *Jane Hall's Big Bad Bus Ride* (ITV)
Film: *Snow in Paradise* (Ipso Facto Films); *Stuart: A Life Backwards* (Neal Street); *The Curry Club* (Sugar & Water Films)

Cary Crankson
Trained at the Royal Academy of Dramatic Art.
Theatre: *Dealer's Choice* (Royal & Derngate/Oxford Playhouse); *Wasted* (Paines Plough/The Roundhouse); *London* (Paines Plough); *Chapel Street* (Underbelly/ Old Vic New Voices); *Othello* (Rose Theatre Bankside); *Mad Blud* (Theatre Royal Stratford East); *Desire Under the Elms* (New Vic Theatre); *Children of Darkness* (Leicester Square Theatre); *The Bitch from Brixton* (The Brockley Jack); *The Rover* (Southwark Playhouse); *The First Domino* (Brighton Theatre); *Oliver/La Ronde* (Riverside Studios and UK Tour); *Rafts and Dreams* (National Theatre Studio); *Swimmer* (National Theatre Studio); *Exit Signs* (Royal Court); *Flight Path* (Out of Joint/ Bush Theatre); *Silverland* (Arcola and 59E59 Theatres, New York); *Thebes, Hamlet, The Robbers, A Midsummer Nights Dream, Othello, Miss Julie, Mary Stuart, Twelfth Night* (The Faction Theatre Company)
Television: *The Bill* (Talkback Thames), *Doctors* (BBC) and *Wild West* (BBC)
Film: *Rock and Roll, F*** 'n' Lovely* (Fish Pot Productions)

Harry Hepple
Trained at the Royal Academy of Dramatic Art.
Theatre: *A Taste of Honey* (National Theatre); *The Lightning Child, Macbeth* (Shakespeare's Globe); *Privates on Parade* (Noël Coward Theatre); *Pippin* (Mernier Chocolate Factory); *A Midsummer Night's Dream, Ragtime* (Regent's Park Theatre); *Hot Mess* (Latitude/ Arcola Theatre); *25th Annual Putnam County Spelling Bee* (Donmar Warehouse); *Jump* (Live Theatre); *Been So Long* (Young Vic/ETT); *Burnt by the Sun* (National Theatre); *I Caught Crabs in Walberswick* (Bush Theatre); *Alaska* (Royal Court)
Television: *Boy Meets Girl* (Pilot, Tiger Aspect); *Holby City, Hustle, Doctors, Inspector George Gently* (BBC); *Misfits* (E4); *Clean* (Pilot)
Short film and recordings: *Been So Long, Strike, Clubland, Absolute Beginners, Life Off, Immersive*

Tendayi Jembere

Theatre: *Romeo and Juliet* (National Theatre); *The Kitchen* (National Theatre); *Angel House* (New Wolsey Theatre, Birmingham REP, West Yorkshire Playhouse); *Mogadishu* (Manchester Royal Exchange, Lyric Hammersmith); *Boy X* (Arc Theatre); *ACTing up!* (Hackney Empire, Manchester Contact, Broadway Barking)
Television: *Kerching!* Series 1-4 (BBC); *Doctors* (BBC); *Mr Harvey Lights a Candle* (BBC); *The Bill* (ITV); *Dubplate Drama* Series Two (MTV, Channel 4)
Radio: *Silver Street* (BBC Asia); *Mogadishu* (BBC Radio 3). Guest presenter on *Rinse FM*

Scarlett Alice Johnson

Theatre: *Slaves* (Theatre503); *Aunt Dan and Lemon* (Royal Court); EPIC (Theatre 503) *Daisy Miller* (National Tour); *Romeo and Juliet* (Stafford Gatehouse); *Under Milk Wood* (National Theatre)
Television: *Babylon* Series One (Channel 4); Playhouse presents NIGHTSHIFT (Sky Arts); *Pram Face* (BBC3); *Big Bad World, Beaver Falls* Season Two (Channel 4); *Pete Versus Life* (Channel 4); *EastEnders* (BBC1); *Freaks, Midsomer Murders* (ITV); *The Damn Thorpes* (Warner Brothers)
Film: *Adulthood, Panic Button, Pimp, The Reed*

Carl Prekopp

Trainer at Central School of Speech and Drama.
Theatre: *Dealer's Choice* (Royal and Derngate); *Roots* (Donmar Warehouse); *The Rover* (Historic Royal Places); *Love on the Dole* (Jagged Fence); *Ruffian on the Stair* (Orange Tree Theatre); *Richard III* (Riverside Studios); *Calendar Girls* (Noël Coward Theatre and Chichester); *Sexual Perversity in Chicago* (Norwich Playhouse)
Television: *Lewis* (ITV); *Law & Order: UK* (Kudos Limited); *Holby Blue* (BBC)
Radio: *Roots, Tommies, The Tempest, The History of Titus Groan, Our Mutual Friend, HMS Surprise, The Worst Journey, The Writer and the Grammarian, My Cousin Rachel, Night Watch, The Brothers Karamazov* (all for BBC)

Matthew Raymond

Trained at The Royal Welsh College of Music & Drama.
Theatre: *Bureau of Lost Discoveries* (Capsule/Birmingham Rep); *The Tempest, Gabriel* (Shakespeare's Globe); *Collisions, Hard Shoulders* (Eyebrow); *Remix* (We Were Here, BAC); *Sold, Even Stillness Breaths Softly* (Theatre503)
Television: *Torchwood* (BBC1); *Dead or Alive* (Sky); *Obsessions* (Sky)
Film: *Rain*

Will Stokes

Theatre: *Busstopkisser* (Camden People's Theatre); *A Clockwork Orange* (Soho Theatre and Australian, UK, Hong Kong and Norwegian Tour); *Hair* (European Tour); *The Wizard of Oz* (Cyprus); *The Medium* (Northern Ireland Tour); *Aladdin* (Camberley Theatre); *The Drowsy Chaperone* (Upstairs at The Gatehouse); *Once Upon a Time at the Adelphi* (Union Theatre); *Peter Pan* (The Leicester Curve); *The Backroom* (The Cock Tavern Theatre); *Jack and the Beanstalk* (Camberley Theatre); *Our House* (Birmingham Rep and UK Tour); *The Thing About Men* (Bedlam Theatre); *Oliver!* (London Palladium)

CREATIVE TEAM BIOGRAPHIES

Matthew Dunster
Director

Matthew is a director, playwright and actor.

Directing includes: *Mametz* (National Theatre Wales); *The Days the Nights the Wounds and the Night* (HeadSpaceDance/Royal Opera House); *Before The Party* (Almeida Theatre); *The Love Girl & The Innocent, You Can Still Make a Killing,* (Southwark Playhouse); *The Sacred Flame* (English Touring Theatre); *A Midsummer Night's Dream* (Regent's Park Open Air Theatre); *Mogadishu* (nominated for Olivier Award for Outstanding Achievement in an Affiliate Theatre, Royal Exchange, Manchester and Lyric Hammersmith); *The Maddening Rain* (Old Red Lion and 59E59, New York); *Love the Sinner* (National Theatre); *The Fahrenheit Twins* (Told by an Idiot and The Barbican); *The Lightning Child, Dr Faustus, Trolius and Cressida, The Frontline* (Shakespeare's Globe); *Saturday Night and Sunday Morning, Macbeth, 1984* (Royal Exchange, Manchester); *You Can See The Hills, Love and Macbeth* (nominated for Olivier Award for Outstanding Achievement in an Affiliate Theatre, Royal Exchange and Young Vic); *Testing the Echo,* (Out Of Joint); *Some Voices, The Member of the Wedding* (Young Vic); *Cruising* (The Bush); *Project B, Project D: I'm Medicore,* The Work; *Port Authority* (Liverpool Everyman); *The Two Gentlemen of Verona,* (Royal and Derngate).

Luke Barnes
Writer

Theatre includes: *Chapel Street* (Underbelly Edinburgh, Bush Theatre, UK Tour); *Bottleneck* (HighTide & Soho Theatre); *Eisteddfod* (HighTide); *Wondrous Place* (Manchester Royal Exchange, Sheffield Crucible, Northern Stage, Northern Spirit); *The Saints* (Nuffield); *Beats North* (Northern Stage and Curious Monkey); *Weekday Nights* (National Youth Theatre); *Geronimo* (Stockton Arc); *Scottstown* (Polokruzba Drovava Theatre, Zagreb); and *Weekend Rockstars* (Hull Truck)

Television includes: *Minted* (C4, Rare Day)

Awards include: *Best New Play* (Runner Up, Off West End Awards 2013); *Most Promising New Writer* (Runner Up, Off West End Awards 2012); *Scotsman Emerging Talent Award* (Winner, Edinburgh 2012); *Old Vic New Voices Edinburgh Award* (Winner, 2012)

Anna Fleischle
Set and Costume Designer

Current work: *John* (DV8 Physical Theatre – National Theatre, NT live and International Tour).

Work includes: Olivier Award winner, Outstanding Achievement in Opera 2014 for *King Priam & Paul Bunyan* (English Touring Opera); *Blindsided* (Royal Exchange, Manchester); *Candide* (Opera National de Lorraine, France); *Before The Party* (Almeida Theatre); *Can We Talk About This?* (DV8 Physical Theatre, Sydney Opera House, National Theatre Lyttleton and International Tour), winner of the Australian Helpmann Award for Best Ballet or Dance Work 2012 (Australia's equivalent of the Olivier Awards) and winner of Production of the Year 2012 Tanz Magazin,

Germany; *Love The Sinner* (National Theatre); *Rats Tales, Saturday Night And Sunday Morning* (Royal Exchange, Manchester); *The Sacred Flame* (English Touring Theatre); *Love And Money* – nominated for the Olivier Awards 2007 for Outstanding Achievement in an Affiliated Theatre (Young Vic and Royal Exchange, Manchester); *The Love Girl & The Innocent* (Southwark Playhouse); *Coram Boy* (Bristol Old Vic at Colston Hall); *Zaide* (Sadler's Wells/Tour); *Troilus and Cressida* (Shakespeare's Globe); *As You Like It* (Curve, Leicester); *Beasts and Beauties* (Hampstead Theatre); *Second Coming* (Scottish Dance Theatre); *You Can See The Hills* (Young Vic/Royal Exchange, Manchester); *Someone Else's Shoes* (ETT and Soho Theatre); *Some Voices* (Young Vic); *Petrushka, Querelle de Brest, In Between There Are Doors, The Bench, 1052* (Badischesstaatstheater, Germany); *Threepenny Opera, Twelfth Night, Pains of Youth* (Theater Erlangen, Germany).

Charlotte Broom
Choreographer

Work as a choreographer includes: *Twelfth Night* and *The Misanthrope* (Liverpool Everyman and Playhouse); *The Lightning Child* and *Macbeth* (Shakespeare's Globe); *Tim Key: A Work in Slutgress* (Edinburgh Festival); *A Midsummer Night's Dream* (Regent's Park Open Air Theatre)

Work as an assistant choreographer includes Bern Ballet and the BBC's *So You Think You Can Dance* (Javier de Frutos)

Charlotte spent twenty years working as a dancer. She was principal dancer at Northern Ballet Theatre and Cullberg Ballet (Sweden) and appeared in numerous productions at Sadler's Wells, the Royal Opera House and in the West End.

As an actor, her work included: *Doctor Faustus* (Shakespeare's Globe) and *Two Gentlemen of Verona* (Royal and Derngate, Northampton)

Charlotte is Co-Artistic Director of HeadSpaceDance.

Emma Laxton
Sound Designer

Current and future credits include: *The Colby Sisters of Pittsburgh* (Tricycle Theatre); *Cat on a Hot Tin Roof* (Royal Exchange Theatre, Royal and Derngate and Northern Stage)

Theatre credits include: *Pests* (Clean Break and Royal Court); *Carthage* (Finborough Theatre); *The Blackest Black, #Aiww: The Arrest Of Ai Wei Wei, Lay Down Your Cross, Blue Heart Afternoon* (Hampstead Theatre); *Coriolanus, Berenice, The Physicists, Making Noise Quietly, The Recruiting Officer* (Donmar Warehouse); *All My Sons, A Doll's House, Three Birds, The Accrington Pals, Lady Windermere's Fan* (Royal Exchange); *Much Ado About Nothing* (Old Vic); *nut* (National Theatre); *Henry The Fifth* (Unicorn Theatre); *OMG!* (Sadler's Wells, The Place & Company of Angels); *There Are Mountains* (Clean Break, HMP Askham Grange); *The Promise* (Donmar Warehouse at Trafalgar Studios); *You Can Still Make A Killing* (Southwark Playhouse); *The Sacred Flame* (English Touring Theatre); *Black T-Shirt Collection* (Fuel UK Tour and National Theatre); *Invisible* (Transport UK Tour and Luxemborg); *Much Ado About Nothing* (Wyndham's Theatre, West End); *Precious Little Talent* (Trafalgar Studios); *Where's My Seat, Like A Fishbone, The Whiskey*

Taster, If There Is I Haven't Found It Yet, 2nd May 1997, Apologia, The Contingency Plan, Wrecks, Broken Space Season, 2000 Feet Away (Bush Theatre); Charged (Clean Break, Soho Theatre); Men Should Weep (National Theatre); My Romantic History (Sheffield Theatres and Bush Theatre); Travels With My Aunt (Northampton Theatre Royal); Sisters (Sheffield Theatres); Pornography (Birmingham Rep/Traverse and Tricycle Theatre); Shoot/Get Treasure/Repeat (National Theatre); Europe (Dundee Rep/Barbican Pit)

Emma is Associate Sound Designer for the National Theatre's production of War Horse and was previously an Associate Artist at the Bush Theatre.

She was previously Deputy Head of Sound for the Royal Court where her designs include: The Westbridge (Jerwood Theatre Upstairs and Theatre Local), The Heretic, Off The Endz!, Tusk Tusk, Faces In The Crowd, That Face (and Duke of York's Theatre, West End), Gone Too Far!, Catch, Scenes From the Back of Beyond, Woman And A Scarecrow, The World's Biggest Diamond, Incomplete And Random Acts Of Kindness, My Name Is Rachel Corrie (Playhouse Theatre, West End and Minetta Lane Theatre, New York and Galway Festival and Edinburgh Festival), Bone, The Weather, Bear Hug, Terrorism, Food Chain (The Royal Court)

Joshua Carr
Lighting Designer
Current & future work includes: Le Gateau Chocolat: Black (Soho Theatre)
Recent credits include: Yellow Face (National Theatre); In The Vale of Health (Hampstead Theatre); All My Sons (Watermill Theatre); Some Girl I Used To Know (West Yorkshire Playhouse and UK Tour); Le Gateau Chocolat: Black (Homotopia Festival, Liverpool and Tour); Unscorched, The Northerners (Finborough); Amygdala (The Print Room); As You Like It (Luxembourg and UK Tour); The Love Girl And The Innocent, Port Authority (Southwark Playhouse); Jekyll & Hyde (Assembly Roxy, Edinburgh and Southwark Playhouse); Yellow Face (Park Theatre); House of Cards (Kensington Palace, Coney); The Miser (Watermill Theatre); President And The Pakistani (Waterloo East); Mansfield Park (UK Tour), Stage Fright (Theatre Royal Bury St Edmunds); One Hour Only (Old Vic New Voices); Mudlarks (High Tide Festival); Dick Whittington (Stafford Gatehouse); His Teeth (Only Connect); Love of A Nightingale, Threepenny Opera, Antigone, A Clockwork Orange (Fourth Monkey); The Song of Deborah (The Lowry); The Shape of Things (Soho Gallery); Cinderella (Young Actors Theatre); Breathing Corpses (Curving Road/Theatre Delicatessen); Billy Elliot (Young Actors Theatre)

As associate lighting designer: Roundabout Season: One Day When We Were Young, Lungs, The Sound of Heavy Rain (Paines Plough and Sheffield Theatres); The Maddening Rain (Brits off Broadway)

As assistant lighting designer: Portobello (Edinburgh); Playing The Games (Criterion); Xerxes (Royal Northern College of Music); Rose (Pleasance); Lake Boat & Prarie Du Chien (Arcola); Lidless (Trafalgar Studios); Ditch (The Old Vic Tunnels).

Dick Straker
Video and Projection Designer
Theatre credits include: *Roots* (Donmar Warehouse); *Paper Dolls* (Tricycle Theatre); *A Marvellous Year for Plums* (Chichester); *Going Dark* (Fuel Theatre); *Tiger Country* (Hampstead Theatre); *The King and I* (Leicester Curve); *Desire Under the Elms* (New Vic Staffordshire); *Seize the Day* (Tricycle Theatre); *Tales of Ballycumber* (Abbey Theatre Dublin); *It's a Wonderful Life* (Wolsey Theatre Ipswich); *The Mountaintop* (Trafalgar Studios); *Rushes* (Royal Ballet); *The Ring Cycle* (ROH); *Sugar Mummies and Hitchcock Blonde* (Royal Court Theatre); *Julius Caesar* (The Barbican); *Richard II* (The Old Vic); *The Woman in White* (Palace Theatre, London and Marquis Theatre, New York); *Henry V, The Coast of Utopia, Jumpers and The Powerbook* (National Theatre).

Dick has designed for many seminal theatre, fashion, commercial and architectural projection events and formed the company Mesmer. He is involved in image production and designing projection that involves creating content for unusual spaces and contexts.

Anna Cooper
Casting Director
As Casting Director:
Nuffield credits include: *A Number, Tonight at 8.30, The Saints*
Theatre credits include: *The Arabian Nights* (Tricycle Theatre); *The Pitchfork Disney* (Arcola); *The David Hare Season* (Sheffield Theatres); *Jeffrey Bernard is Unwell* (Theatre Royal Bath & tour); *Ghosts* (West End); *The Fastest Clock in the Universe* and *Lucky Seven* (Hampstead Theatre); *Educating Rita* (Watermill Theatre); *Measure for Measure* (Theatre Royal Plymouth & tour); *Our Country's Good* (Liverpool Playhouse); The High Tide Festival (2007); *Scenes from An Execution* (Hackney Empire); *'Tis Pity She's A Whore* (Southwark Playhouse)
Short film credits include: *Act of Love* and *That Woman*
Radio credits include: *Skyvers* and *The Reluctant Spy*
As Casting Assistant:
Television credits include: *Atlantis; Silk; Vicious; The Politician's Husband; Best of Men; George Gently VI; We'll Take Manhattan; Doc Martin; Outcasts; Ashes to Ashes; Benidorm; Gavin & Stacey; Mutual Friends; Wild At Heart; Trial & Retribution* and *Harley Street*
Film credits include: *Belle; The Dark Knight Rises; Fast Girls; Ashes; Sex and Drugs and Rock 'N' Roll; Poppy Shakespeare; Mr. Nobody; Largo Winch; Pope Joan; The Other Boleyn Girl* and *Angel*
Theatre credits include: *The Curious Incident of the Dog in the Night-Time* (National Theatre); *Privates on Parade* and *Peter & Alice* (Michael Grandage Company); *The Real Thing, Six Degrees of Separation* and *Dancing at Lughnasa* (Old Vic Theatre); *The School for Scandal* (Theatre Royal Bath); *A Delicate Balance, The Master Builder, Hedda Gabler, Festen, The Goat, or Who is Sylvia, Whistling Psyche, Push: Two Step, The Earthly Paradise, Macbeth, Blood Wedding, Romance* and *The Hypochondriac* (Almeida Theatre) and *The Birthday Party* (Lyric Hammersmith).

THE SAINTS

Luke Barnes

THE SAINTS

OBERON BOOKS
LONDON

WWW.OBERONBOOKS.COM

First published in 2014 by Oberon Books Ltd
521 Caledonian Road, London N7 9RH
Tel: +44 (0) 20 7607 3637 / Fax: +44 (0) 20 7607 3629
e-mail: info@oberonbooks.com
www.oberonbooks.com

A catalogue record for this book is available from the British
Library.

PB ISBN: 978-1-78319-155-0
E ISBN: 978-1-78319-654-8

Cover design by Farrows Creative

Printed, bound and converted
by CPI Group (UK) Ltd, Croydon, CR0 4YY.

Visit www.oberonbooks.com to read more about all our books
and to buy them. You will also find features, author interviews and
news of any author events, and you can sign up for e-newsletters
so that you're always first to hear about our new releases.

This book is to say thanks to T, Sam Hodges and Matthew Dunster. And is for anyone who's ever stood on some terraces hoping for something amazing to happen.

'My favourite theatre is Old Trafford'
Sarah Kane

'Everything about life I learnt from football'
Bill Shankly

Characters

KENNY

EMILY

MUM

JOEY

JEREMY MCCARDLE

CARL

JOHNNO

COLIN

DAVE

COMMENTATOR 1

COMMENTATOR 2

GRANDSTAND VOICE

GEORGINA

SARAH JANE

DOCTOR

MATT LE TISSIER

FRANCIS BENALI

FANATIC

CLOWN

DAD

VICAR

TED BATES

CHORUS

OUTSIDE

There are people trying to sell spare tickets, people selling merchandise, hot dog stands and programmes…drunken knobheads, tourists and fanatical religious figures making use of the crowd.

INSIDE

We're in a stadium complete with scoreboard, seating, dug-outs and advertising.

There is a section, like a directors' box, of the theatre full of football fans that KENNY and the crew sit with during the matches.

The actors are warming up. When they're not taking part they sit in the dug-out with the stage manager.

COMMENTATOR 1: Hello and welcome to Radio Solent tonight *(Whatever date and year it is.)* where we're going to be live at Nuffield Playing Field at Guildhall Square for the highlights of Kenny Glynn, the world's biggest Saints fan and world's least successful Sunday league footballer, taking on the world here in Southampton. Keep an eye on the scoreboard for how he's getting on. Might be useful to tell everyone Wrighty. How did this all start?

COMMENTATOR 2: Well we're about to find out –

Peep. Kick off.

The actors all jump into action.

Our highlights begin at the beginning. In 1996 at Kenny Glynn's first visit to the Dell!

Act One

1996

KENNY and his DAD are watching Southampton beating Manchester United 4-3). KENNY is on his DAD's shoulders.

COMMENTATOR 1: What's going on here then?

DAD has to put KENNY down.

COMMENTATOR 2: Our hero Kenny Glynn is watching as The Saints take apart Manchester United 4-3

The Saints score a goal.

COMMENTATOR 2: Sorry 5-3, my mistake.

COMMENTATOR 1: And who's that with him?

His DAD has to sit down.

COMMENTATOR 2: That's his father, Mr Glynn.

COMMENTATOR 1: He does not look well, does he.

COMMENTATOR 2: Not at all.

His DAD throws up.

COMMENTATOR 1: Kenny does not look happy about that, he doesn't know what to do.

His DAD passes out.

KENNY: Help! Help! Help!

KENNY can't take his eyes off the footy.

COMMENTATOR 2: Oh poor kid he can't take his eyes off the footy.

The Saints score their last goal.

COMMENTATOR 2: GOALLL. 6-3.

KENNY is distracted from his DAD and, as the first aiders turn up, he keeps watching the game.

COMMENTATOR 1: Poor lad.

DAD is stretchered out… KENNY stays and watches, until the peep, peep, peep. Then he chases his DAD.

GOAL: KENNY 0 – THE REST OF THE WORLD 1

1997
JUNIOR SAINTS
END OF COURSE PARTY

KENNY 4 – THE REST OF THE WORLD 38

A Saints-themed pervy CLOWN takes centre stage and sings a song, all the kids are in 90s training kits, shirts etc… Sportswear –

CLOWN: OK everybody that's the end of the summer soccer school. I've loved helping out and as a result I've got the football bug. I'm starting a junior football team– if anyone wants to join, tell your parents to let me know – it's Sarah Jane's dad if you can't tell in the costume. OK everybody – join in and do the dance with me…

He sings 'Barbie Girl' by Aqua and does a dance, some of the kids join in, some of them don't.

COMMENTATOR 1: 1997. A party to celebrate the end of the junior Saints soccer school and the birth of the Millbrook Saints, which ties our heroes together. For some reason Sarah Jane's dad has taken it upon himself to organise the party and dress up as a clown. Weird.

COMMENTATOR 2: But this boy dancing like a chicken will grow to be the biggest Saints fan in the world. There's no one else – if Pompey have Mr Pompey, Newcastle have that topless fat guy, then Southampton has Kenny Glynn. What a lad.

KENNY: I'm gonna kiss Emily under the table.

JOEY: That's disgusting.

KENNY: You're disgusting. I've been watching the porn. There's loads worse than kissing under the table.

CLOWN: OK boys and girls. What can I do now? Do you think I can make this disappear?

KIDS: No!

CLOWN: I beg your pardon?

KIDS: No!

CLOWN: OK but if I can… You have to all join in my dance. OK?

KIDS: OK!

CLOWN: OK?!!

KID: OK!!!!

CLOWN: Great.

The pervy CLOWN performs the most amazing magic trick of all time.

KIDS: Wowwww!

CLOWN: OK kids. Let's go. Everybody follow me. 5-6-7-8.

The kids go mental and don't follow it. The CLOWN can't keep them under control. KENNY doesn't join in.

EMILY: You OK?

KENNY: Yeah. Fine.

EMILY picks up some food and throws it at him. He throws some back. They have a little food fight. Everyone joins in. The CLOWN loses control. He breaks down in the corner and starts crying. All the kids jump on him.

KENNY: … I like your hair.

EMILY: Thanks.

KENNY: … I like your nose as well.

EMILY: Thanks. Bye.

EMILY turns around and walks away and helps beat up the CLOWN.

KENNY: Emily?

EMILY: What?

KENNY: I drank a whole pint of milk and threw up on the floor yesterday.

EMILY: What do you want?

KENNY: I er… I…

COMMENTATOR 1: 'And this is it. It's Le Tissier vs Flowers. The biggest penalty of Kenny's life so far…'

KENNY: *(To EMILY.)* I love you. I'm gonna be a footballer one day and I'm gonna need a WAG. Can we get married and have babies and one day I can take you on a holiday to France and we can sit in a tent and kiss all day and share a toothbrush and have sex?

EMILY: Why would we share a toothbrush and have sex?

KENNY: Because that's what love is… Love is sharing a toothbrush and love is the same as sex. Why you looking at me like that? It is. Isn't it? My dad loves Saints so that means he has sex with Saints right? That's what you do when you're in love. Right so I'm in love with you so that's mean we should have sex.

He goes in the corner.

Let's start.

He drops his trousers

A group of girls – 'ewwwwww' etc…

KENNY 4 – REST OF THE WORLD 39

KENNY: *(To audience.)* There is no worse combination than standing at a party with your trousers down, thirty kids and a clown laughing at your willy and your mum walking in to tell you your father's died.

Mum Kenny. Come on.

EMILY gives KEN a party bag to cover himself up with.

KENNY: Emily I…I…

He's sick on her feet. The girls all go ewwww.

KENNY 4 – THE REST OF THE WORLD
40 – 41 – 42 – 43

KENNY: *(To audience.)* Nothing will ever go worse than this.

MUM'S KITCHEN 1998

KENNY 9 – THE REST OF THE WORLD 118

COMMENTATOR 1: It's 1998 and Kenny Glynn is the man of the house now.

COMMENTATOR 2: The Glynns look weak as a team without their star striker.

MUM: You not going out again?

KENNY: No.

MUM: Do you not want to play with ya mates?

KENNY: No.

MUM: It's ya birthday, ya should be out with them not here with me.

KENNY: Everyone's gone Quazar and they know I'm afraid of the dark.

MUM: Could they not have done something you enjoy for your birthday?

KENNY: Are you gonna take me the dell then?

MUM: Stop asking me this Ken, you know I can't.

KENNY: Why not?

MUM: It's very expensive.

KENNY: I don't get it, dad took me.

Beat.

KENNY: Do you miss dad?

MUM: Eat your broccoli.

KENNY: No. I'm pissed off.

MUM: Why?

KENNY: Who did Saints play week before last?

MUM: I've forgotten, who?

KENNY: I've forgotten too. What if we just forget Dad?

MUM: We won't.

KENNY: But what if we do?

MUM: We won't.

KENNY: Can I go the match then?

MUM: No.

KENNY: I've got it all figured out, I leave at 12, I can walk five minutes to the bus stop, get the 12.12 bus into town that takes thirty minutes and be there by 12.42 to get into the ground for 1 o'clock and I'll be back by 3.50.

MUM: No.

KENNY: Pleassseee.

MUM: No.

KENNY: Please!

MUM: Will ya stop bothering me?

KENNY: Yes.

MUM: Then alright. But don't come running to me when you get murdered.

KENNY: Thanks Mum. Where are you going?

MUM: Hold on.

She goes off and comes back with a present.

KENNY: What's this?

MUM: Dad's birthday present to you. He left it in the wardrobe.

KENNY unwraps it, it's a Saints Scarf.

It's his, from the '76 cup final.

KENNY 10 – THE REST OF THE WORLD 118

Read the card.

KENNY: 'Dear Kenny, Happy Birthday, I always wanted to go back to Wembley with you and now this is probably the closest I'll get. Love you very very much. I'll see you at the match. Dad x'

MUM: Happy Birthday. Put it on. The next time they get to Wembley I promise I'll pay for you OK? I promise that. I can't afford to pay for you every week like daddy did but I can promise that. OK?

KENNY: You OK Mum?

MUM: Yeah.

KENNY: It's OK Mum.

MUM: I'm sorry. Will you promise me something?

KENNY: Yes.

MUM: I want you to do everything you want Ken. Yano like… like Matt Le Tissier never misses a penalty. He always takes his chances. Is that what you say? Is that right?

KENNY: I love you.

MUM: I love you too Ken. Now eat your broccoli. I'm going to bed. I don't feel well. Happy Birthday.

KENNY: Thanks Mum.

She goes.

KENNY: *(To audience.)* I remember thinking there is as much chance of us going to Wembley as there is of mum being happy.

COMMENTATOR 1: You can't choose your family and before there was Sky ya couldn't choose ya football club.

COMMENTATOR 2: Kenny's inherited his love for the club from his father and it's going to make him a legend of the Glynn household.

COMMENTATOR 1: Hold on what's going on here?

COMMENTATOR 2: I think he's gone to Emily's house. Oh dear this could be embarrassing.

KENNY knocks on the door. EMILY answers. She's playing her song. She switches it off.

EMILY: What?

KENNY: Hi Emily. I er… I just wanted to say sorry about the party.

EMILY: What party?

KENNY: Sarah Jane's party, last year, where I was sick on your feet.

EMILY: What?

KENNY: Where the pervy clown did the magic trick and then we danced with him and then I was sick?

EMILY: I don't know what you're talking about?

KENNY: You know… When my…yano. You gave me the party bag. Last season.

EMILY: Why you saying season?

KENNY: Year.

EMILY: Oh when you were naked?

KENNY 10 – THE REST OF THE WORLD 119

KENNY: Yeah.

EMILY: Yeah. What do you want?

KENNY: I've been thinking about you giving me the party bag, it was really nice. I've been thinking about it loads and now Dad's dead I just thought I should say all the things I want to in case I never get to say them. I wanted to say thank you and wanted to ask you…

EMILY: Oh yeah, maybe, I mean… Yeah. Sure. It's fine.

KENNY: I feel really embarrassed about it. What's the matter? Are you going through menopause? My mum gets that. I understand it – let me give you the massage I give her. Come here.

EMILY: Get off.

KENNY: Get on all fours and breath.

EMILY: Why are you here?

KENNY: I was just… I was just wondering if you wanted to come to mine tomorrow after school and play FIFA?

EMILY: I'm busy tomorrow.

KENNY: What you doing?

EMILY: Guides.

KENNY: How about Tuesday?

EMILY: I'm busy then.

KENNY: What you doing?

EMILY: St John Ambulance with Kelly.

KENNY: How about Wednesday? People don't do much on Wednesdays so it might be nice to relax.

EMILY: I'm busy.

KENNY: You do something the first three nights of the week?

EMILY: Yeah.

KENNY: Well what do ya do on Wednesdays?

EMILY: Netball. I've got to go Mum's made tea.

KENNY: What ya having?

EMILY: Oven baked smilies and chips with peas.

KENNY: OK great. Well I'll knock next weekend. See ya then.

EMILY: I'm busy.

KENNY: Cool. I'll save you a place in assembly.

EMILY: I sit next to my friends in assembly.

KENNY: Cool. Lunch then. See ya then.

EMILY: I eat lunch with friends.

KENNY: Great I'll meet you at the gates after school.

EMILY: What are you doing?

KENNY: I'm taking a penalty.

EMILY: Ken it's not that you're not nice it's just… You're weird.

KENNY: I just want to hang out with you.

EMILY: Maybe some other time.

She goes.

KENNY: YES! SOME OTHER TIME!

KENNY 11 – THE REST OF THE WORLD 119

She wants to see me another time! GET IN! *(To audience.)* If you don't keep shooting, you'll never score a goal. One day Emily will be my girlfriend and from this point on – Emily is my FA Cup and I am Southampton.

TRAINING:
MILLBROOK AFC YOUTH RESERVES

COMMENTATOR 1: The boys have just finished training and are having a kick about.

COMMENTATOR 2: The one to watch is this boy Joey, in the red top and Adidas predators.

JOHNNO: No I wouldn't be good with Sarah Jane because Sarah Jane's boobs are too big. When I'm famous I'm gonna get a girl with big ones but not like that big, just like perfect big.

COLLIN: You can't buy a girl with bigger boobs.

JOEY: You can buy anything you want when you're a footballer.

JOHNNO: Yeah.

COLLIN: You can't buy girls.

JOHNNO: No. That's true.

JOEY: But you can definitely get fitter ones.

JOHNNO: You can.

JOEY: And ones with bigger boobs.

JOHNNO: Yes.

KENNY: Emily's got none but I still fancy her because she's got the best face. And she's kind. And she has that little thing when she smiles. And when she walks it's always like she's going somewhere like this… She never just… Walks. I think she'd be a good ref, I know she can't be a player because she's a girl but she'd be a good ref. She's the sun and the stars and when I sleep I dream of her, I've written a poem about her: wana hear it?

You are the balls to my feet,

The goal to my volley,

The whistle to my mouth.

You are the game Emily

And I am the player.

What do you think? I was thinking about giving it to her in geography but I'm a bit scared. What do you think?

The lads are all silent.

KENNY: What? What's the matter?

JOHNNO: Collin's been getting with her.

KENNY 11 – THE REST OF THE WORLD 120

KENNY: How long for?

COLLIN: Few weeks. Unlucky.

KENNY: Why didn't you say anything?

COLLIN: Why should I? You don't need to know every girl I'm getting with do ya.

KENNY: Are you her boyfriend?

COLLIN: No. Don't want to be now do I.

KENNY: I haven't kissed her or anything.

COLLIN: No but you've made her not fit by fancying her haven't you.

KENNY: No she's more fit for me fancying her because she won't go out with me. She's like the FA Cup and I'm a conference team. I mean you're division one of course.

COLLIN: I'm premiership. And stop being gay.

KENNY: Yes Collin I'm a massive gay. I love to kiss boys and hold hands with them in the woods. I might even want to kiss you.

COLLIN: Don't even joke about that.

KENNY: Alright – I'm just saying I liked her since that soccer school thing.

COLLIN: Well. Whatever. She's mine now isn't she.

KENNY: Fine. Whatever.

COMMENTATOR 1: It's all getting a bit heated down there on pitch level.

COMMENTATOR 2: It's going to need the level head of captain supreme.

JOEY: Lets not argue. Let's talk about me. When I grow up I'm going to be super fly when I leave the academy and when I graduate I'm going to play for the first team. I'm gonna stand there in the middle and be like YEEEAAHH. And everyone's gonna clap like YEAHH and I'm gonna get my mum on the pitch and give her a kiss on the cheek and make everyone clap her. Then I'm gonna buy everything, I'm gonna buy cars and houses and I'm gonna Bargate and I'm gonna buy the Marina and I'm gonna buy the University. That's what I'm gonna do, I'm gonna buy the university and let all my mates who can't earn money like be able to go there for free. That's what I'm gonna do. It's gonna be sick. Yeah. That's it. Yeah.

COLLIN: Do you know how many footballers don't make it?

JOEY: I don't care about players that don't make it. I care about those who do. We made Alan Shearer, Matt Le Tissier, Alan Ball, Terry Paine, Alf Ramsey, Charles Miller… Matt Oakley! If I was ever going to make it I'm in the right place.

JOHNNO: I can't wait for you to be a footballer.

KENNY: And when I'm a footballer I'm gonna –

COLLIN: You're not gonna be a footballer.

KENNY: Why not?

COLLIN: If you were gonna be a footballer then you'd have been spotted like Joey.

KENNY: Ian Wright didn't get discovered till he was in his twenties so there's time. I'm gonna buy my own football team and play myself because I'm great.

JOHNNO: Yes Kenny. I'm gonna be a coach for your team and get them to the premiership.

They high five.

DAVE: I'm going to be an air steward.

Beat.

COLLIN: What?

DAVE: I'm gonna be an airsteward.

JOHNNO: Coz you're gay?

DAVE: I'M NOT GAY

Beat.

JOEY: Made friends with the tickets people because I'm at the academy didn't I. So we can get tickets.

KENNY: Can I come?

JOEY: If you pay.

KENNY: You'd make me pay?

JOEY: I'm not a charity am I.

KENNY: Fair enough.

COLLIN: Why did you stop going? Because your dad died?

KENNY 11 – THE REST OF THE WORLD 121

KENNY: Let's play.

JOEY: 2 on 2

The lads break into a game.

JEREMY MCARDLE walks past with a dog.

JEREMY MCARDLE: Alright boys. Nice ball. Easy boy. Easy

COMMENTATOR 1: Kenny is still holding a grudge because Jeremy McArdle laughed as he drove past in the car on the way to his dad's funeral. That was a year ago. He's been carrying it around ever since.

JEREMY MCARDLE: Don't look him in the eye.

COMMENTATOR 2: Kenny hates him more than life itself.

JEREMY MCARDLE: Can I play?

JOEY: No.

JEREMY MCARDLE: Why not?

JOEY: Because it's team training and you're not in the team.

JEREMY MCARDLE: Kenny let me play.

KENNY: I dunno Jeremy, it's not my ball.

JEREMY MCARDLE: Whose ball is it?

KENNY: Dunno.

JEREMY MCARDLE: Fine. I don't want to play anyway. Gays. Come on Alan. Laters.

JEREMY MCARDLE walks away.

KENNY 12 – THE REST OF THE WORLD 121

KENNY: *(To audience.)* It's getting late. The sun's setting and we're about to go home.

COLLIN: We're off. Laters losers. Yeah I'm not bothered about Emily anyway. I like Sarah Jane. She likes sailing. You're both mings, you can have her. You got any beconase?

DAVE: Yeah.

COLLIN: Cheers – laters losers.

JOHNNO and COLLIN leave.

KENNY: I can't believe she's seeing him, you know he looks like Egil Ostenstad.

JOEY: Bit harsh

DAVE: I'm off.

JOEY: See ya.

KENNY: See ya later Dave.

DAVE: Yeah. See ya. Don't say I'm gay again I'm not, people always say it and it annoys me ok? If they say it again will ya send up for me please? It's like someone talking about your dad. … Sorry it's just…sorry.

KENNY: Sorry.

DAVE: Ok. I'll see ya later.

DAVE leaves.

JOEY: Sorry about Emily mate.

KENNY: I'll get her eventually.

JOEY: Yeah. See ya later. Hope ya mum's feeling better.

KENNY: What?

JOEY: Yano.

KENNY: No I don't know what are you talking about?

JOEY: My dad told me.

KENNY: Told you what?

JOEY: What?

KENNY: I don't know what you're talking about.

JOEY: Forget I said anything it's just my dad chatting shit. I'll see you later. You out tomorrow?

KENNY: … Yeah. Yeah course I am.

JOEY: Cool I'll knock for ya then.

KENNY: Alright cool.

They hug. But they negotiate it like MEN.

JOEY goes.

Some football action happens in KENNY's game against life and we're with MUM trying to get up the stairs…

INSIDE KENNY'S MUM'S HOUSE

MUM climbs the stairs, it's difficult.

KENNY: *(To audience.)* I miss dad.

COMMENTATOR 2: Shame the veteran isn't here to tell him what to do.

COMMENTATOR 1: That's not something you want to see at a football match.

KENNY: You alright Mum?

MUM: Fine.

KENNY: You want some help?

MUM: Just having a little sit. You go and play.

KENNY: Joey says you're ill.

MUM: I'm just… Just go to your room.

KENNY: Are you ill?

MUM: I'll be fine.

KENNY 12 – THE REST OF THE WORLD 122

KENNY: Do you want me to get you a hot water bottle?

MUM: No it's alright. I'll be alright the morning, just go to bed.

KENNY: OK. Night night.

INSIDE KENNY'S BEDROOM

KENNY dresses as a fairy.

COMMENTATOR 1: And this is odd behaviour from young Kenny Glynn.

COMMENTATOR 2: There's no chance his manager told him to do that. He's gone mad.

COMMENTATOR 1: Why's he doing this?

KENNY: Show yourself.

MATT LE TISSIER appears with Angel Wings.

23

KENNY: Hello…

GOD (AS MATT LE TISSIER): Hi.

KENNY: Where's…?

GOD (AS MATT LE TISSIER): I'm your guardian angel – but I'm dressed as Matt Le Tissier. What do you want?

KENNY: Just wanted to chat Matt.

GOD (AS MATT LE TISSIER): I'm not Matt – I'm your guardian angel… I'm just dressed as Matt Le Tisser.

KENNY: Why?

GOD (AS MATT LE TISSIER): He's your hero.

KENNY: OK.

GOD (AS MATT LE TISSIER): … Great. Anything you want in particular?

KENNY: I want some advice.

GOD (AS MATT LE TISSIER): OK. About what?

KENNY: You know…

GOD (AS MATT LE TISSIER): I don't know

KENNY: You do, you're supposed to be my guardian angel.

GOD (AS MATT LE TISSIER): Kenny I've goct a lot going on, I'm looking after like 1,000,000 people.

KENNY: Are you Matt Le Tissier to everyone?

GOD (AS MATT LE TISSIER): No.

KENNY: Who else are you Matt Le Tissier to?

GOD (AS MATT LE TISSIER): Just to you and a couple of England managers but they're all idiots. Now what do you want?

KENNY: I want to be like Joey, I want to be the best footballer in our team so that everyone will love me in school and I want Emily to think I'm the greatest thing in the world. How do I get it?

GOD (AS MATT LE TISSIER): Right. Well. I'll start with a question. Do you know why the people of Southampton love me?

KENNY: Because you've been here for ages?

GOD (AS MATT LE TISSIER): Yep. Do you know why I've been here for ages?

KENNY: Because Southampton made you rich and famous?

GOD (AS MATT LE TISSIER): No.

KENNY: Because you're a team player?

GOD (AS MATT LE TISSIER): No Kenny.

KENNY: I dunno then.

GOD (AS MATT LE TISSIER): Because I'm always here for the club. And it's not about me. As a player and as a fan, it's always about the city and the club And that's how you get what you want Kenny – by being there for other people, playing for them not for yourself and then when the time comes they will be there for you. And that's how you get your friends to love you. As for the girl – that's down to luck – it's like a football team, no one wins anything without working together, good luck and a selfish individual who likes to bang it in from 40 yards. That's not you Kenny. That's me. I'm the brilliant individual. You need to be a team player.

KENNY: Emily will love me.

GOD (AS MATT LE TISSIER): Sure she will. But if she loved you for being the best footballer like Joey or me it wouldn't be love would it, she'd just love the idea of you. Good lad. Go and see your mum. When the things we love are struggling, all we can do is be there. See ya later.

KENNY: Matt?

GOD (AS MATT LE TISSIER): Yeah?

KENNY: Thanks.

GOD (AS MATT LE TISSIER): It's alright mate

MATT LE TISSIER disappears. He goes to his mother.

KENNY 13 – THE REST OF THE WORLD 122

KENNY: *(To audience.)* If I can support a team like Saints I can support my mum. With both I hope better days are coming.

GRANDSTAND VOICE: Millbrook Saints vs. Northam Locals

KENNY and his mates line up in their Millbrook Saints kits

Peep.

The game happens. KENNY runs for everything, chases people down, works his arse off but ultimately lost balls and lack of fitness lose them the game.

Peep.

GRANDSTAND VOICE: Millbrook Saints 1 Northam Locals 32

2001. SOUTHAMPTON VS. ARSENAL. THE LAST GAME AT THE DELL.

KENNY 13 – THE REST OF THE WORLD 497

COMMENTATOR 1: Kenny is down 13 to 497. Gabby Logan. Welcome.

COMMENTATOR 2: Thank you.

COMMENATOR 1: Maybe you can tell us why today is so special.

COMMENTATOR 2: Well. It's four years later and Kenny and his mates have all saved up for the last game at the Dell.

The Stadium changes to the Dell.

A FANATIC: Lads. Lads. It's written in this book – Do not mourn the passing of the old. Do not mourn it for it is written if anyone is in Christ, he is a new creation… Think of that today as we say good bye… God Bless Stuart Grey, God Bless Ted Bates, God Bless all the Saints and let us bare them in mind as we Behold the new. *(He spots KENNY.)* I know you're listening. In the Darkness we need this, in death we find God and I promise mate, I promise that the good times are coming back. Not just in football. Even though the Dell is going good times are coming. Christ rose from his grave and so will we – we just have to have faith –

Someone has shut him up.

Give me back my microphone!

KENNY 13 – THE REST OF THE WORLD 498

KENNY: Sailing?! Colin & Johno have gone sailing? They've sacked off the last ever game at the Dell to sit on a bit of wood in the water?

DAVE: Yeah. Gays.

JOEY: You say that too much I think Dave.

KENNY: Not coming here is like turning down sex for a yogurt. Let's go in.

KENNY's phone rings.

MUM: Where are you?

KENNY: I'm at the dell Mum.

MUM: Can you get some toilet paper from the shops?

KENNY: I'm not gonna be back for hours.

MUM: Oh. OK.

KENNY: Do you want me to go now?

MUM: It's not urgent.

KENNY: Right.

MUM: I'm alright. I'm fine.

KENNY: Don't worry I'll go.

MUM: No…

KENNY: I'm going Mum.

MUM: Kenny it's fine.

KENNY: I'll get some now.

MUM: Oh don't worry –

KENNY: Na it's fine mum. Honestly.

MUM: No don't worry.

KENNY: It's fine. I'll go now.

MUM: It's alright Ken. Enjoy the match I can sort myself out.

KENNY: I'll come back.

MUM: Kenny come back and I'll be pissed off OK. I can sort myself out. It's not urgent. It was just if you were passing. Go and enjoy the match.

KENNY: Are you sure Mum?

MUM: Yes. I'm sure.

KENNY: OK Mum.

MUM: I'll see you later.

KENNY: See you later.

INSIDE THE DELL

COMMENTATOR 1: The atmosphere here is palpable, you can taste it and it tastes like 15,000 excited people waiting to see some football.

COMMENTATOR 2: And here they are, finding their seats on the little wooden benches to take it all in.

They take their seats in the audience, there's an empty seat next to them.

KENNY: *(To audience.)* For the last 100 years we've been walking up and down that road, going to the same pubs, walking in to the dell, looking at the same sky, looking at those same red and white shirts, hoping for something to set Saturday on fire in this spot where all the little towns of Southampton come together and as it's going I want you to remember this, remember all the people that have passed through these gates and remember that your dad went through the same gate and his dad did and his dad did and his dad, we've all stood or sat where you're sitting now and that's what this club is, it's not who's wearing the shirt on the pitch, it's not this old stadium, it's the people sitting there, it's us, it's this ritual and it's this city. There's football and that's it. It's about tradition, it's about keeping the spirit of this town alive.

JOEY: I can't believe we're here.

DAVE: Thanks for inviting me guys.

JOEY: No worries mate.

KENNY: You're about to witness magic Dave.

JEREMY MCARDLE comes in and sits next to them with his DAD.

KENNY 37 – THE REST OF THE WORLD 500

KENNY: Oh cock.

JEREMY MCARDLE: Dad this is Kenny and his mates.

JEREMY MCARDLE'S DAD: Kenny Glynn?

KENNY: Yeah?

JEREMY MCARDLE'S DAD: How's ya mum? This is exciting isn't it Jeremy?

JEREMY MCARDLE: I love going to football with you.

COMMENTATOR 1: This must be awful for Kenny.

COMMENTATOR 2: A game his father would have loved.

Peep. The game kicks off.

We're observing the last ever game at The Dell, just as KENNY is from the stands.

KENNY: *(To audience.)* At first the game is slow and I'm looking at the bench at the over-weight, over-age man with the big nose sitting on it and I know, I just know deep down in my Soton veins that I am about to see a piece of history and that that history will involve that man. But meanwhile…

First goal.

KENNY: Ashley Cole beats it down the left wing, bangs a shot, saved…and then…

Ashley Cole scores.

JOEY: Ashley Cole. Balls.

COMMENTATOR 1: And that's not the start we were hoping for.

COMMENTATOR 2: Not at all. Kenny looks upset.

Second goal.

KENNY: Giles Grimandi gives the ball away at right back.

JOEY: Kachoul.

KENNY: Kachoul has the ball

KENNY: YESSS!!!!

DAVE: Look he's saluting like a sailor!

JOEY: 1-1

COMMENTATOR 1: Kenny looks happy with that.

COMMENTATOR 2: Things are looking brighter for Ken.

Third goal.

KENNY: Thierry Henry blitzes it down the right wing plays it in and NO FREDDIE LLUNGBURG. Right. Come on.

COMMENTATOR 1: Dangerous amount of tension in Kenny Glynn.

Fourth goal.

KENNY: The ball's played high in the air, it sort of…scrambles and…and…Kachoul pokes it in the net. Right. COME ON!

COMMENTATOR 2: That's the Kenny we like to see.

MATT LE TISSIER comes on.

KENNY: Oh. My. God. And here he is, the Crown King of Southampton, the Dean of the Dell, the G of Guernsey, the Chief of the Channel Islands and the stadium goes mental as the ball is played up the field from Jones, it falls in the area, falls lose and…OH MY GOD MATT LE TISSSIEEEEERRRRR!!!!

The stadium goes mental.

The noise of the crowd is deafening and ecstatic.

KENNY 38 – THE REST OF THE WORLD 501

Everyone rushes the stage – a big banner saying R.I.P. Dell

The LADS jump around hugging each other.

COMMENTATOR 1: Southampton is on fire.

The place goes mental. And the boys are taken out by the stewards.

OUTSIDE THE DELL

They hug. COLLIN and JOHNNO have come down to soak up the atmosphere.

COLLIN: Look at this.

KENNY: Get in.

COLLIN: You're alright.

JOEY: Get in lads.

JOHNNO: Shall we?

DAVE: Oh come on lads get in the cuddle, huddle!

COLLIN: … Alright.

Everyone's hugging.

LADS: Yay!!!

KENNY 39 – THE REST OF THE WORLD 501

Then, like a mirage, appears EMILY.

KENNY 40 – THE REST OF THE WORLD 501

KENNY: Emily!

EMILY: Oh. Hi Ken. How's it going?

KENNY: Good yeah. Did you see the footy?

EMILY: Na I'm just meeting a friend. See ya then.

KENNY: I had three WKDs before I went in. They're my mum's but she don't know I'm pissed. Mad me. Pissed.

EMILY: Right. Bye.

KENNY: Listen I wanted to ask ya.

EMILY: Not now Ken, go enjoy this with ya mates.

KENNY: Please.

EMILY: No, you're too pissed.

KENNY: Na I was just that saying that to impress ya. I'm not pissed, look I'll prove it.

EMILY: You don't have to prove it.

He stands on one leg and holds his ear.

EMILY: Great. Did you think I'd be impressed by WKDs?

KENNY: Yeah. No. Do you wana go the pictures on Friday?

EMILY: Ken –

KENNY: I've got vouchers to the Odeon.

EMILY: I can't.

KENNY: Free slush puppies when you buy a hot dog.

EMILY: I can't.

KENNY: Why not?

EMILY: Ken you're being weird, it's cringe.

KENNY: It's the simplest thing in the world. It's not weird it's honest. I just want to go out with you.

JEREMY MCARDLE approaches. Puts his arm around EMILY.

KENNY 40 – THE REST OF THE WORLD 502

JEREMY MCARDLE: Everything alright Ken? How's ya mum?

KENNY: Great Jeremy. She's great.

JEREMY MCARDLE: Has he asked you out?

EMILY: ….

JEREMY MCARDLE: HAHAHAHAHA. Great.

KENNY 40 – THE REST OF THE WORLD 503

KENNY: Great. See ya later.

COMMENTATOR 1: And that has to hurt.

KENNY: I hate him more than anything else in the world.

COMMENTATOR 1: Can't see Kenny getting up from that one.

JOEY: Let's buy season tickets.

DAVE: In.

JOHNNO: In.

KENNY: In.

KENNY 41 – THE REST OF THE WORLD 503

COLLIN: You can't get any.

KENNY: Joey'll sort us. I'm gonna save up. I'm not missing any games. Ever.

JOEY: Collin. You in?

COLLIN: … Pricey.

KENNY: Yeah but you can't put money on these experiences can ya.

COLLIN: I'll think about it.

KENNY: Come on.

COLLIN: I said I'll think about it.

JOEY: Right ignore him he's being difficult. Let's go get pissed!

LADS: Wahay! Lads, lads, lads, lads

KENNY: *(To audience.)* This is going to be so good. A new stadium is built right by St Mary's Church where it all started.

Some people come on and transform The Dell to St Mary's. He keeps seeing EMILY.

KENNY: All the builders were from Portsmouth and what they did was they buried a Portsmouth top right under the pitch. Right here. And everyone thought the stadium was cursed. So this happened.

Someone dressed as a witch doctor comes on and does a de-curse dance.

KENNY: This guy de-cursed it. And then it was ready to go, look at it, it's perfect.

The first time I walked to St Mary's I realised why it was here. You can see the church in the distance, that church where a hundred odd years ago men started playing footy before prayers and it evolved into this, this cathedral. And to get here form the city you have to walk by the docks or through industrial areas and there's something perfect about that. There isn't a spot on earth that would be more perfect for my Saints to play their football.

And we marked it's opening by playing Espanyol. And we were there!

LADS: Yeah! Lads, lads, lads.

KENNY: They beat us 4-3. But we were here. With the Saints. At St Mary's.

2002

KENNY 81 – THE REST OF THE WORLD 946

COMMENTATOR 1: 2002 and we're in the pub after training.

JOEY: I've done it

KENNY: Done what?

JOEY: Got a contract.

KENNY 82 – THE REST OF THE WORLD 946

DAVE: What?

JOEY: I'm joining the reserves.

COLLIN: How did that happen?

JOEY: What do you mean?

COLLIN: You're shit, I was better than you.

JOHNNO: Shut up man, we're all buzzing for ya Joey.

KENNY: It's amazing mate.

DAVE: Yeah honestly.

COLLIN: It's amazing. Fucking… Made up for ya.

JOEY: Do you know what this means lads? If this all goes well none of you will ever have to work, none of you will have to worry that you've bollockesd your GCSES, I'm gonna buy a massive house and we can all live in it.

JOHNNO: Can we get birds back?

JOEY: Yes mate.

JOHNNO: What? Strippers?

JOEY: Suppose so mate.

KENNY: Is it gonna be like Ayia Nappa? *(Sings 'A Little Bit of Luck'.)*

JOEY: It's gonna be better mate.

DAVE: What's the first thing you gonna do?

JOEY: Now? Celebrate.

IN A CLUB

COMMENTATOR 1: It's like a jungle here Wrighty.

COMMENTATOR 2: Yeah. It's wicked.

KENNY: *(To audience.)* Can't believe we got in. It's full of underagers this is amazing. This is the Millbrook Saints toasting one of our own leaving us and going professional. Nothing can ruin this. Nothing can make this night shit for us…

EMILY's song is playing

KENNY: This is Emily's song.

IAN WRIGHT: This one goes out to all the love makers.

JEREMY MCARDLE: and EMILY are kissing and dancing around the stage.

KENNY 83 – THE REST OF THE WORLD 947

KENNY: *(To audience.)* No. Nothing's gonna ruin this.

GEORGINA is watching KENNY.

I know who that is. I know who that is. I shouldn't but… Standing tall, chest out, ginger hair and she's looking at me, and seeing that… I …I… Can't help myself. Oh God. Oh balls.

KENNY and GEORGINA dance. They move into kissing. They move into theatrical sex… And then in comes COLLIN.

COLLIN: What the fuck are you doing?

GEORGINA runs away.

COLLIN: Go home or I'm telling mum.

KENNY: I don… I'm sorry.

COLLIN: That's my sister.

KENNY: –

COLLIN punches him.

KENNY 83 – THE REST OF THE WORLD 948

COMMENTATOR 1: Oh my god that was brutal. Can we see it again?

The punch replays and then the whole club erupts into a scrap.

KENNY'S MUM'S HOUSE

KENNY, with a black eye, goes into his room and dresses as a fairy.

COMMENTATOR 1: It's hard to iron out these bad habits in young players.

COMMENTATOR 2: It would appear so yes, suppose he hasn't had chance to break the habits of his childhood never leaving home.

KENNY: Show yourself.

GOD (MATT LE TISS): Alright Ken?

KENNY: I'm worried.

GOD (MATT LE TISS): About what?

KENNY: I'm scared I'm gonna be doing this forever. I'm scared I'll never move on. I'm scared I'll never get Emily. I've just got in a fight because of something I did because I can't get over her.

GOD (MATT LE TISS): What do you think Franny?

FRANNY BENALI appears.

GOD (FRANCIS BENALI): Well. Lawrie McNememy, when he managed The Saints, had a philosophy that was passed down through the club – and that was…you need a load of road sweepers and a couple of violinists. By which I mean you need hard workers and a couple of geniuses. That's society right.

GOD (MATT LE TISSER): He also said that you need young lads to be the legs and old lads to be the brains. So here's what we're gonna do. You're gonna be the legs and we're gonna be the brains.

KENNY: Whose gonna be the violinist?

GOD (AS MATT LE TISSIER): You.

KENNY: And you're the road sweeper?

GOD (FRANNY BENALI): No that's you as well.

KENNY: OK.

GOD (AS MATT LE TISSIER): What would you do?

KENNY: Me?

GOD (FRANNY BENALI): Yeah. If you were us and we were you. What would you say to us?

KENNY: I dunno.

GOD (AS MATT LE TISSIER): Go on. What would you tell us to do?

KENNY: Tell her how you feel.

GOD (FRANCIS BENALI): Do that then.

KENNY: I've been telling her since we were eleven and she keeps turning me down.

GOD (AS MATT LE TISSIER): All you have to do, is wait for her options to match your face. Do you know what I mean?

KENNY: No.

GOD (AS MATT LE TISSIER): Right. OK. Women's options run out quicker than men's. So their standards are bound to drop. Maybe this girl's standards have dropped enough to match your head? If you know what I'm saying.

KENNY: Maybe – yeah.

GOD (FRANNY BENALI): Great I'm off.

GOD (AS MATT LE TISSIER): See ya.

KENNY: See ya. Thanks for the… chin up.

He goes.

GOD (AS MATT LE TISSIER): What you gonna do?

KENNY: I'm gonna wait til her standards have dropped.

GOD (AS MATT LE TISSIER): Good lad.

GRANDSTAND VOICE: Millbrook Saints v Shirley Little Giants

Peep.

Shirley Little Giants Score.

Peep.

GRANDSTAND VOICE: – Millbrook Saints 3 – Shirley Little Giants 12.

2003

KENNY 140 – THE REST OF THE WORLD 1869

KENNY: *(To audience.)* We're going to go through the next bit at a bit of a lick, because to be honest I don't really want to dwell on it – it's just twelve years of hurt and disappointment.

COLLIN: I've slept with your cousin.

KENNY: Alright.

KENNY 140 – THE REST OF THE WORLD 1870

EMILY: We're gonna wait til we're twenty-one – then I'm going to marry Jeremy

KENNY 140 – THE REST OF THE WORLD 1871

KENNY: OK that hurts.

JOEY: I'm gonna be a superstar Ken. Look at me. Everything is brilliant.

KENNY 141 – THE REST OF THE WORLD 1872

KENNY: Nice one. You still gonna play with Millbrook on Saturday? First game of the season?

JOEY: Can't be doing that mate. Not now I'm a pro.

KENNY: Oh right. OK. *(To audience.)* We win no games anyway.

MUM: I think it's time I got a part-time job. Before I get too ill. I wanna work.

KENNY: OK Mum.

KENNY: *(To audience.)* And that's how everything is. This man.

GORDON STRACHAN: Hello.

KENNY: Gordon Strachan. Gets us an 8th place finish. We reach an FA Cup Final but I couldn't take Dad's scarf to Wembley because it was on in Wales and I couldn't go anyway because I had glandular fever. We lost to Arsenal 1-0. Great. I re-sit my GCSEs and fail and I'm doomed to work in Tesco's unless Joey makes it and I become part of his entourage. My idol at this point is this man.

JAMES BEATTIE: Hello.

KENNY: James Beattie.

KENNY 142 – THE REST OF THE WORLD 1871

Wow.

2004

KENNY 171 – THE REST OF THE WORLD 2159

KENNY: A year later naturally the good football's gone out of the window as this man, this man –

GORDON STRACHAN: Hello.

KENNY: ...resigns.

GORDON STRACHAN: Goodbye.

KENNY: And was replaced by this man.

PAUL STURROCK: Hello.

KENNY: That's Paul Sturrock by the way. We finish 12th and go out of the league cup in the second round, the FA cup in the first round and our long awaited return to Europe ends after one game. It's like someone made you a cake and then threw it on the floor before you could eat it. It's like life, you can see the life you want but you can never quite get it.

JEREMY: Alright babe listen I've got to tell you something. I've been seeing someone else.

EMILY swills him.

KENNY: Yes!

KENNY 172 – THE REST OF THE WORLD 2159

KENNY: Emily. Do you wana go for a drink?

EMILY: No. I'm having a break from men.

KENNY 172 – THE REST OF THE WORLD 2160

KENNY: You can see the life you want but you can never quite get it.

JOEY: Another year Ken and we can move out of our mum's and you can stop working in Tesco's.

KENNY: Yes Joey!

JOEY: How are the Millbrook Saints getting on without me?

KENNY: Not great.

JOEY: You won any yet?

KENNY: No.

KENNY 172 – THE REST OF THE WORLD 2161

KENNY: But it's not the winning, it's the taking part that counts isn't it.

COLLIN: Kenny.

KENNY: Yeah?

COLLIN: That's too far.

KENNY: What do you mean?

COLLIN: Don't talk to my mum on Facebook yeah. That's not funny.

KENNY: It's just a joke.

COLLIN: Mums. It's not funny. You know that as well as anyone.

KENNY 172 – THE REST OF THE WORLD 2162

MUM: What is it then?

DOCTOR: We think it's progressive supernuclear palsy which can cause a Parkinsonism – but the onset can be very slow.

KENNY 172 – THE REST OF THE WORLD 2163

KENNY: What happens now?

DOCTOR: Her vision, movement and speech will slow and deteriorate.

MUM: What can I do?

DOCTOR: Take the medication and hope for the best.

MUM: Right.

KENNY: If I can be there for Saints I can be there for her. If my new hero –

JAMES BEATIE: Hello.

KENNY: – James Beattie – Can be our top scorer two years in a row with a head that big, I can do anything.

2005

KENNY 211 – THE REST OF THE WORLD 2846

KENNY: The glory days are over. This is our last season in the premiership. And despite efforts from three different managers –

PAUL STURROCK: Hello.

KENNY: Paul Sturrcok

STEVE WIGGLY: Hello.

KENNY: Steve Wiggly

HARRY REDKNAPP: Hello.

KENNY: Harry Redknapp. And despite Redknapp signing this gangly no mark.

PETER CROUCH: *(Does 'The Robot'.)*

KENNY: Peter Crouch. After twenty-seven years we're relegated to the championship, suddenly we're with small clubs with amazing fans and a part of me feels at home – I see myself in these people. And these things happen.

MUM: We're going on holiday Ken. I want to start doing things before it gets too late.

KENNY: Alright.

EMILY: Hi.

KENNY: Emily hi. What's up?

EMILY: Nothing, you don't want to hear my problems.

KENNY: Na go for it.

EMILY: I've been seeing this estate agent and he's been sleeping with his secretary.

KENNY: Oh no. Wana go for a drink?

EMILY: I'm leaving Ken. I'm going to Portsmouth to work in my auntie's shop.

KENNY 211 – THE REST OF THE WORLD 2877

EMILY: I'll see you soon.

KENNY: Oh OK.

COLLIN: I've got your hamster.

KENNY: What?

COLLIN: Hidden it in the woods.

KENNY 211 – THE REST OF THE WORLD 2878

KENNY: I hate you Collin!

DAVE: I think we should have a chat.

KENNY: About what?

DAVE: Where we wana carry on Millbrook Saints or not.

KENNY: Of course we do.

DAVE: But it's no fun when we lose.

KENNY: It's exercise Dave, we all need it.

JOEY: I'm making my debut tomorrow against Crewe Alexandra.

KENNY 212 – THE REST OF THE WORLD 2878

JOEY makes his entrance. Everyone cheers. And in the game he breaks his leg. Everyone is mortified.

KENNY 212 – THE REST OF THE WORLD 2879

KENNY: And with that it all disappears. I'll never be a part of his entourage. I'd put all my dreams into someone else. I'm an idiot. This is me forever.

2006

KENNY 236 – THE REST OF THE WORLD 3318

KENNY: And in 2006 we're at a standstill. Emily still in Portsmouth and I haven't seen her for ages. Collin has started throwing cans of Cherry Cola in my mum's garden and I know it's him because he's the only person whose mum buys Cherry Cola.

KENNY 236 – THE REST OF THE WORLD 3319

And Mum wants to go travelling but we haven't got loads of money so we can only go in the UK. Here's us at Stonehenge.

There it is.

KENNY 237 – THE REST OF THE WORLD 3319

KENNY: And Joey won't go and watch the games – because he can't bear to see the life he would have had. Hey Joe.

JOEY: Yeah?

KENNY: You wana come manage Millbrook?

JOEY: No.

KENNY 237 – THE REST OF THE WORLD 3320

KENNY: OK. This man –

HARRY REDKNAPP: Hello.

KENNY: Quits because this man –

SIR CLIVE WOODWARD: Hello.

KENNY: Sir Clive Woodward is brought in as technical support director. And so Redknapp is replaced by this man –

GEORGE BURLEY: Hello.

KENNY: George Burley. Who becomes our seventh manager in six years. And to make things worse. Nothing happens. We finish twelfth. I'm starting to think nothing will ever change. Maybe this is what life will be like forever. Mid table championship finishes and fish finger dinners. Nothings changing. And I'm scared because I can't see anything else.

2007

KENNY 252 – THE REST OF THE WORLD 3708

KENNY: And we have a whole season with the same manager! Mum and me go to Buckingham Palace for the day. Here we are.

There they are.

KENNY 252 – THE REST OF THE WORLD 3709

KENNY: Collin admits to the Cherry Coke cans so I start putting cheese slices on his car, not loads, just one a night and his mum has a go at my mum and we fall out proper.

KENNY 252 – THE REST OF THE WORLD 3710

We reach the semi finals of the play offs and I think for the first time we're going back up but we don't. Again. We go to penalties at Derby and a player we signed from Derby, Inigo Idiakez, misses our last penalty – putting them through to the final. How dodgy is that??

KENNY 252 – THE REST OF THE WORLD 3711

KENNY: The life we want is always this close but we can't get it. It's a carrot we can't reach and we're just dogs pushing shopping trolleys around Tesco's.

Emily's still in Portsmouth. Joey's still not going the games. Millbrook Saints still haven't finished above last place. And I'm still hoping.

2008

KENNY 293 – THE REST OF THE WORLD 4481

KENNY: Mum and I go to Paulton's Park and have an awful time because she couldn't go on any rides and it's really expensive. We didn't take any photos. I follow Emily on Facebook and she's still in Portsmouth dating some new man. Anyway – this man –

GEORGE BURLEY: Hello.

KENNY: George Burley. Leaves for this man –

JOHN GORMAN: Hello.

KENNY: John Gorman. Who leaves for this man –

NIGEL PEARSON: Hello.

KENNY: Nigel Pearson. Who becomes our ninth manager in eight years. And we finish twentieth in the flippin' Championship. The Saints are nearly on the point of oblivion. And a part of me is thinking that I am too. And Joey won't go to games. And Collin still hates me. And we had to ask Dave's dad's mates to play for Millbrook Saints because people were dropping out. All in all. Bad year. But things are going to get worse.

2009

KENNY 321 – THE REST OF THE WORLD 5619

KENNY: 2009. This man –

NIGEL PEARSON: Hello.

KENNY: Nigel Pearson. Leaves – and this man –

JAN POORTVIELTE: Dag.

KENNY: Jan Poortvielte. Takes over, only to be replaced by this man –

MARK WOOTE: Dag.

KENNY: Mark Woote. Who became our eleventh manager in ten years. And we go down to division 1. On the last day. A new low. This is the darkest day of my life. Emily's nowhere to be seen. Colin tells me he hates me and means it.

COLIN: I hate you –

KENNY: – and means it, Joey won't even talk about football –

JOEY: Shut it –

KENNY: – and I got –

DOCTOR: – chicken pox.

KENNY: And my mum doesn't want to go away anymore. And we had to down Millbrook Saints to a five-a-side team. As Southampton freefall, so do I. And I don't know what to do. All I can do is turn up every week in my red and white and hope that something's going to change.

At the start of the 2009-2010 season we have a handicap.

GRANDSTAND VOICE: Southampton Leisure Holdings PLC have entered administration. As a result Southampton FC will begin the season with a ten point deduction.

The ADMINISTRATOR turns up.

KENNY 321 – THE REST OF THE WORLD 5620

We're in Division 1 and we're at Huddersfield. Mum's still ill.

… and she is

KENNY 321 – THE REST OF THE WORLD 5621

Collin still hates me

… and he does

KENNY 321 – THE REST OF THE WORLD 5622

Emily is nowhere to be seen.

KENNY 321 – THE REST OF THE WORLD 5623 (SCORE THEN INCREASES EVERY 3 SEC)

ADMINISTRATORS: You're in debt.

KENNY: And we are in debt, with no manager, no chair and no owner.

This is the lowest we've ever been.

Out of nowhere – MATT LE TISSIER turns up.

KENNY: Pinnacle. Matt Le Tissier and The Ex-Saints in all their glory try to save our club.

MATT LE TISSIER prepares to fight.

KENNY: But then these men –

MARKUS LIEBHER: Guten Tag

KENNY: Marcus Liebher –

NICOLA CORTESE: Ciao

KENNY: Nicola Cortese. Appear from nowhere.

MARKUS LIEBHER and NICOLA CORTESE defeat THE ADMINISTRATOR.

KENNY 431– THE REST OF THE WORLD 3010

KENNY: Like a blind dog puts all its faith in its owner I put all mine in these men Markus Liebher and Nicola Cortese and they not only sort out all the debt – but with the help of this man –

ALAN PARDEW: Hello.

KENNY: Alan Pardew. They win us one of these –

Someone lifts the JPT Trophy

LADS: Yeahhhh!!!

KENNY 432 – THE REST OF THE WORLD 3010

KENNY: The Johnson's Paint Trophy. Although I couldn't go to take Dad's scarf back to Wembley because I had shingles and Joey got upset about not being able to play anymore so I stayed with him. And let's be honest – The Johnson's Paint Trophy – just doesn't count.

KENNY: On the 11 August 2010 Markus Liebherr, may he rest in eternal peace, dies,

KENNY 432– THE REST OF THE WORLD 3011

and nineteen days later Pardew is shown the door.

ALAN PARDEW: Which way?

KENNY: That way, mate. And then this man –

NIGEL ADKINS: Hello.

KENNY: Nigel Adkins. Takes us up to the Championship. And at the start of the next season we hold the memorial cup for Markus Liebherr and then this man.

NIGEL ADKINS: Hello.

KENNY: Who is my new hero takes us back in the Premiership where we belong!

LADS: Yeahhhhh!

KENNY 433– THE REST OF THE WORLD 3011

KENNY: And it's going great. Joey gets is getting over his accident and has got a new job.

JOEY: I'm a brickie now. It's great.

DAVE: I'm gonna study.

JOHNNO: I work in a call centre.

COLLIN: I'm a postman.

KENNY: And I decide I've had enough of Tesco's so I buy I taxi, well I say I buy a taxi, this man –

JOSEF ABDULLAH: Hello.

KENNY: Josef Abdullah whose dad owns the curry house at the end of our street buys it, and I use it when he's sleeping. But all's going alright until this man –

MAURICIO POCHETTINO: Hola.

TRANSLATOR: Hello.

KENNY: Mauricio Pochettino. Comes in and we hate him – because him being here means Adkins wasn't. But then we realise he's brilliant –

MAURICIO POCHETTINO: Eso Esel Futbol

TRANSLATOR: That's football

KENNY: – and he gets all our hopes up. Then this man leaves.

NICOLA CORTESE: Arrivederci

KENNY: So does this man –

MAURICIO POCHETTINO: Adios

TRANSLATOR: Goodbye.

KENNY: And then the vultures fly over St Mary's and start picking off the stars form our team Rickie Lambert, Adam Lallana, Luke Shaw. They all go. Leaving us with nothing. My friendship with Collin is nothing. Joey feels like he's nothing. Mum has nothing to look forward to. My prospects are nothing. We have nothing.

KENNY'S MUM'S HOUSE – 2014

KENNY 352 – THE REST OF THE WORLD 8832

COMMENTATOR 1: Kenny has been working all day and he looks knackered doesn't he Wrighty.

COMMENTATOR 2: Not a good a look, the stress has taken its toll, maybe it's time for a sleep.

His MUM's going out.

KENNY: You alright mum?

MUM: I've got you a present.

KENNY: What really?

MUM: Yeah.

KENNY: What for?

MUM: Why not?

KENNY: Where is it?

MUM: Over there.

… It's a poor imitation of the 1976 away kit.

KENNY 353 – THE REST OF THE WORLD 8832

MUM: It's the 1976 away kit. Knitted it myself.

KENNY: Thanks Mum. It's beautiful.

MUM: You gonna wear it to the match?

KENNY: Yeah Mum. Course. Wow.

MUM: Listen. I wanted to have a chat with you.

KENNY: About what?

MUM: I want you to be happy, you know that don't you?

KENNY: Yeah.

MUM: OK. So bear in mind that I love you when I'm saying this. OK. OK?

KENNY: Yeah.

MUM: I'm going on a date.

KENNY 471 – THE REST OF THE WORLD 3357

KENNY: What about Dad?

MUM: I don't know how long I'm going to be able to do things and I… I can't have you looking after me forever. Ken –

KENNY: You're finding it hard get up the stairs, how are you going to go on dates?

MUM: I want you to go out and meet nice girls and bring them home, I want you to chase your dreams, I want all of those things for you and you can't do them unless I'm independent. And I want to be. So I'm going on a date. And you'll have to get used to it.

KENNY: I just want you to be happy mum.

MUM: And I want you to be. That's why I'm doing this.

KENNY: Should I ask who he is?

MUM: His name's Carl and he's a nurse.

KENNY: Great.

MUM: I want to have someone else Ken, I rely on you too much and I really like him.

KENNY: How did you meet him?

MUM: At the doctor's.

KENNY: Great.

MUM: I want you to meet a girl Ken, you've spent too much time with me. You look handsome tonight.

KENNY: Shut up – really?

MUM: Yes.

KENNY: You think I've lost weight?

MUM: You looked the best you've looked in years.

KENNY: Really?

MUM: Yeah.

KENNY: Thanks mum.

MUM: Do you know who I saw today?

KENNY: Who?

MUM: That Emily girl with her mum in Tesco. The one from your class.

KENNY: Oh. Right. Don't even remember her.

MUM: You do.

KENNY: Mum?

MUM: What?

KENNY: You look really nice. Have a nice time.

COMMETANTOR 1: And we're coming up to half time here in the game of Kenny Glynn's life but there's two minutes added time.

COMMENTATOR 2: Has he got it in him to pull one back.

KENNY: *(To audience.)* I go on Facebook and I click to see what Emily's doing. She's moved back to Southampton. Interesting. I click to see what she's doing. Florist. Interesting. I click on the florist to see where it is. Down the road. Interesting. I click to see what time it's open. Until 6. Interesting… I look at her status "I've had it with losers. All the best men are already married. The next good man I meet, I'm marrying!" Interesting…. Liebher took a massive risk with us and he made a lot of people happy. Maybe I should take a risk… Fuck it.

FLORIST

EMILY is behind the counter with another girl. KENNY enters. He's nervous.

EMILY: Kenny? Kenny is that you?

> *... KENNY is sick into a flower pot and runs away. Leaving behind a CD.*

KENNY 353 – THE REST OF THE WORLD 8833

GIRL: Who was that?

EMILY: No one. Just this boy I used to fancy at school.

They play the CD. It's her song.

EMILY: Omg this is my song.

She follows him. He's in his cab. With a fare.

EMILY: Kenny.

KENNY: Get out mate.

MAN: Really?

KENNY: Yeah it's booked.

MAN: But you said –

KENNY: Na sorry mistake. *(He pretends his phone rings.)* Hello? Yes. *(To MAN.)* Sorry mate it's central office I have to take this girl, OK bye.

He gets out. She gets in.

KENNY: Oh god I'm really sorry about the sick.

EMILY: Don't worry about it, it's just a spider plant.

KENNY: Yeah but it's covered in sick now.

EMILY: Don't worry about it. You alright?

KENNY: Yeah. Yeah I'm fine.

BOTH: Listen. Would you like to go for a drink?

KENNY 472 – THE REST OF THE WORLD 3358

EMILY: Sure, be nice to catch up.

KENNY: I mean, would you like to go for a drink? A drink with me. Tonight. Like. A drink? Drink.

EMILY: Oh.

KENNY: Fuck it. I knew you'd say no, you're still too good for my face. I shouldn't have listened to them.

EMILY: What? No it's not that –

KENNY: It's fine. I get it, you don't want to be with a man like me I understand, it makes sense it defies…biology or something like us winning the FA cup I get it.

EMILY: Ken – if you let me finish. I haven't got anything to wear.

KENNY: What's wrong with that? You look beautiful.

EMILY: What this?

KENNY: Yeah.

EMILY: Really?

KENNY: You could turn up in a bin bag and I'd still think you were beautiful.

EMILY: You're very sweet.

KENNY: You look lovely. What time do you finish?

EMILY: Six.

KENNY: I'll pick you up here at six.

EMILY: OK.

KENNY: OK. Cool. See you then. Babe. Sorry about the er… Sorry about the sick. See ya.

She gets out of the cab.

EMILY: See ya.

He drives away.

KENNY: Yeah!

He scores a goal against life.

KENNY 354 – THE REST OF THE WORLD 8833

The crowd go mental.

HALF-TIME

COMMENTATOR 1: Ladies and Gentlemen welcome to the half-time show. Put your hands together for: Sammy Saint and Super Saint

The two giant dogs do a clown act.

Act Two

JANUARY 2015 FA CUP 4th ROUND. SOUTHAMPTON vs. ROTHERHAM.

KENNY 479 – THE REST OF THE WORLD 9502

COMMENTATOR 1: Wow. Here we are. 2015 and a lots changed hasn't it Wrighty.

COMMENTATOR 2: It sure has. Let's have a look. Here we are – at the Chapel Arms.

CHAPEL ARMS

JOEY and KENNY are at the bar.

KENNY: There's no chance we're winning today they've got David Moyes and he's somehow made them play like Barcelona.

JOEY: Don't know why Moyes went to Rotherham.

KENNY: No one else wanted him did they.

JOEY: It's your birthday though so we can hope can't we.

KENNY: Fair enough.

JOEY: Happy Birthday

JOEY gives him a present.

KENNY: Cheers mate.

JOEY: Don't open it now, wait for the others.

KENNY: Alright. Nice one.

JOEY: I think it's our year Ken.

KENNY: Why?

JOEY: Just got a feeling?

KENNY: You got a feeling about Saints? You mad?

JOEY: Well it has to be our year.

KENNY: Why does it have to be our year?

JOEY: That's how history works.

KENNY: What do you mean that's how history works?

JOEY: Cycles.

KENNY: What do you mean cycles?

JOEY: In history who always loses?

KENNY: I dunno mate, who always loses?

JOEY: Winners lose Kenny. They have to. It's our turn. £50 we win something.

KENNY: This is Southampton mate. We don't win stuff.

JOEY: We have to Ken I'll go mad otherwise.

KENNY: You wana calm down mate.

JOEY: What do you mean calm down you're the one who cried when we sold Luke Shaw.

KENNY: I'm not bothered now me, got a bird, suppose Saints is just a thing to fill the gaps when you've got nothing else on.

COMMENTATOR 1: And player manager Kenny Glynn steps through the tunnel into the main area of the Chapel Arms where he's met by a thunderous applause from his co players.

COMMENTATOR 2: Here are The Millbrook AFC Youth reserve Old Boys at home in their best formation.

LAD: Lads.

KENNY: Where's my birthday pints then?

Silence.

DAVE: I'm broke mate. Just paid my tuition fees.

JOHNNO: And me, only doing part time on the phones now.

JOEY: And me Ken, sorry.

COLLIN: I'm not buying you a pint if no one else is.

KENNY: … So no one's gonna buy me a pint on my birthday?

Silence.

KENNY: Fair enough I'll get me own.

KENNY 479 – THE REST OF THE WORLD 9503

KENNY comes back with a pint.

JOEY: To Ken's birthday and to the swan song Season of the Millbrook Saints!

LAD: Hurray

JOHNNO: Karaoke?

KENNY: Yeah mate. Go on. Sing me a birthday song.

JOHNNO: Alright. But open the present first.

He opens the box and a big poo falls out.

KENNY 479 – THE REST OF THE WORLD 9504

LADS: Lads. Lads. Lads. Lads.

JOHNNO: This one's for Ken, his fit bird and despite being ill, his even fitter mum.

JOHNNO goes over to the karaoke stand and starts to sing a power ballad.

KENNY's phone rings

Emily's ringing me. I love her even when she said:

EMILY: I've been with 113 men.

KENNY: And

EMILY: One of them was Mr Pompey.

He answers the phone

Hi Love. Yeah sure. I'll see you later. Just off the match.

He hangs up

KENNY: *(To audience.)* This is what we live for. We live to get messed up, out of heads, high as kites. This is what going the game is. Going the game is getting out of our minds. And I love it.

LET'S GO!

THE MATCH – SOUTHAMPTON Vs. ROTHERAM

We're now watching Southampton play. The footballers swarm the stage.

CROWD: We're Northam, We're Northam, We're Northam over here….

COMMENTATOR 1: And here we are at Southampton Vs. Rotherham.

COMMENTATOR 2: Kenny's got it all. Sitting in the Northam end with his mates and several thousand angry Saints fans.

COMMENTATOR 1: They're partying like they've something to celebrate – this is terrible.

COMMENTATOR 2: Terrifying. Let's see what the Saints can do.

KENNY: Who's starting?

JOEY: Navas

KENNY: Can't believe we got him from Bayern.

JOEY: Can't believe he's been so shit since the World Cup.
Navas.
Clyne
Fonte
Chambers
Rio Ferdinand – nearly went to QPR. Nailed it.
Schneiderlin *(Captain)*
Ward-Prowse
Cork
Wanyama
Tadic – he scored 1 every 2 last year for FC Twente. Why's he so shit for us?
and
Rodregues
Good team I reckon. Money well spent. Thank you Catherine Liebherr.

KENNY: We're gonna get battered. We're already going to get relegated and now we're gonna get knocked out of the cup by Rotherham.

JOEY: Shut up man. Ronald Koeman. That's all you've got remember two words. Ronald Koeman.

KENNY: Against David Moyes? No chance.

JOEY: Fonte I feel it.

KENNY: If Fonte scores I will get Le Tiss and Benalis face on my arse.

JOEY: You mean it?

KENNY: Yeah.

JOEY: You're on.

KENNY: Clyne breaks down the right. He crosses in – JAMES WARD PROWSE. Ohhh

COMMENTATOR 1: Kenny nearly wet himself

KENNY: Phew.

This is boring and OH MY GOD JOSE FONTE 40 YARDS. YEAHHHHHHHHHH!

Saints win 1-0.

COMMENTATOR 1: Kenny Glynn is delighted with that.

KENNY 480 – THE REST OF THE WORLD 9504

JOHNNO: How did the Pompey do?

COLLIN: 2-1 Carlise.

DAVE: Fish Face. Bastards

JOEY: You made a promise mate.

KENNY: It was a joke.

JOEY: Come on.

The tattooist comes on.

KENNY: No!!!!

He gets tattoos of Matt Le Tissier and Benali on his bum.

KENNY 480 – THE REST OF THE WORLD 9505

HOME

COMMENTATOR 1: And here we are again and he's...and he's doing this again.

COMMENTATOR 2: Yes I. I don't really know what to say about it any more.

KENNY dresses as a fairy

KENNY: Show yourself!

The GUARDIAN ANGEL appears.

GOD (AS MATT LE TISSIER): Hello Kenny.

KENNY: Hello.

GOD (AS MATT LE TISSIER): You with us Ted?

GOD (AS TED BATES): Hello?

KENNY: Hello

GOD (AS MATT LE TISSIER): There we go. This is Kenny.

GOD (AS TED BATES): Hello Kenny

KENNY: Who are you?

GOD (AS TED BATES): I'm an Angel. Dressed as Ted Bates. Can't you tell?

KENNY: Why are you silver?

GOD (AS TED BATES): Would you recognise me if I wasn't?

KENNY: No.

GOD (AS TED BATES): There we go then.

KENNY: Right.

GOD (TED BATES): What can I do for you Ken?

KENNY: I just wana say thank you for your guidance. This is the happiest I've been in my life. I've got money, looking after Mum, got Emily, Saints are doing well. Thank you.

GOD (TED BATES): Hmmmm.

KENNY: What do you mean hmmm?

GOD (TED BATES): Well yano... Be careful.

KENNY: What do you mean?

GOD (TED BATES): Well… When we won the cup we were on top of the world right but er… That's not life is it. In life you're tested and that's the mark of a man – enjoy the good times and be ready because it's in losing them all that you become a man. That's how you know a good player see – when they lose they come back harder.

Life turns on KENNY. He manages to hold them off.

KENNY 481 – THE REST OF THE WORLD 9505

KENNY: Whatever.

GRANDSTAND VOICE: Millbrook Saints Vs. Chillwall Rovers

Peep.

GRANDSTAND VOICE: Millbrook Saints 3 – Chillwall Rovers 3

THE MATCH – SOUTHAMPTON Vs. CHELSEA. FA CUP 5th ROUND.

COMMENTATOR 2: Kenny's looking nervous

COMMENTATOR 1: Don't like to see him like this. He's been wanting this since he was born – win this and we're one big step closer to Wembley.

COMMENTATOR 2: Hopefully the Saints can give him something to cheer about.

COMMENTATOR 1: We of course go into this game with the sad news that John Terry has had to retire from football after a broken leg inflicted on him by Yaya Toure and Vincent Company in a scene that resembled Bash Brothers from Mighty Ducks. And here we go. Southampton Vs. Chelsea.

We're watching Southampton Vs. Chelsea.

JOEY: We're going out here mate, there's no point watching. Wanyama is gonna get nailed by Eden Hazard all day.

KENNY: Shut up.

KENNY: AHHHHHHHHHHH Rodregues. Rodregues. Rodregues. Yes yes yes. Come on.

JOEY: Hazard. Ah! Hazard. Ah! Hazard Ah! Oh my god I'm going to have a heart attack.

DAVE: Tooorrrresssss

KENNY: Yes Navas. He's amazing.

COLLIN: Oh my god Navas has hands like a piranha.

KENNY: A what?

COLLIN: Shut up you look like a baby bell.

JOHNNO: Come on. 10.9.8.7.6.5.4.3.2.1…

Peep peep peep

Southampton 1–Chelsea 0

LADS: WHAHAHAY

KENNY 482 – THE REST OF THE WORLD 9505

COLLIN: How did the gil heads do?

They look to the scoreboard…

GRANDSTAND VOICE: Portsmouth 3 Rushdon 0

DAVE: Bastards.

KENNY: We might get them in the next round.

JOEY: Who we got?

They look at the screen… Leeds.

JOEY: Fuck. We should take that.

DAVE: Who have Portsmouth got?

They look at the Screen…. Oldham

JOEY: Arseholes. Wana get fucked?

KENNY: Yes mate! *(To audience.)* I've not heard from Emily for days. It's alright. Seeing her for Brunch tomorrow. Minimal work. Life is fucking good.

KENNY does a pill. Snorts a couple of lines. Necks a beer and goes dancing. The Theatre turns into a rave.

COMMENTATOR 1: It's not nice to see this is it Wrighty?

WRIGHTY is raving.

COMMENTATOR 1: Wrighty? Wrighty? Wrighty?! WRIGHTY!

COMMENTATOR 2: No it's not let's hope that by tomorrow he will have forgotten it.

Life turns up and plays against KENNY, KENNY's so fucked they just keep scoring.

The Millbrook Saints line up. Hung-over. One of them might even throw up.

COMMENTATOR 1: Millbrook Saints Vs. Weston Warriors

Peep.

GRANDSTAND VOICE: Millbrook Saints 1 – Weston Warrior 32

BRUNCH

COMMENTATOR 1: Varsity does jacket potatoes for £4.95. Is that what he's gone for?

COMMENTATOR 2: Certainly is. She's got a tap water. Does not bode well. No one ever ordered a tap water and nothing else before saying anything good and at seven months into the relationship you'd expect her to at least be getting some onion rings so he doesn't feel bad about eating alone.

KENNY: How's ya water?

EMILY: You look like shit. You're hung over aren't you.

KENNY: A bit. What you doing this afternoon?

EMILY: You're taking the mick. I spent all Saturday working and you're at the game getting drunk.

KENNY: Hey you choose ya job ya not me.

EMILY: You're twenty-nine, what are you doing with your life?

KENNY: You've been talking to your mum again haven't ya.

EMILY: Course I've been talking to her, I live with her. Most of my mates are living with their fellas.

KENNY: Thought we were waiting til we're ready?

EMILY: I need you to make a choice.

KENNY 482 – THE REST OF THE WORLD 9506

KENNY: What do you mean you need me to make a choice?

EMILY: I need you to make a choice between me and The Saints.

KENNY: What Southampton or Millbrook?

EMILY: All of it. I need you to choose between me and Southampton Football Club. And your mates. And getting tattoos on your bum of men with weird faces. I need a man who's going to be there at weekends with me and the kids not going to the match and coming back with tattoos.

KENNY: Kids?

EMILY: One day yeah… I want a family Kenny and not with a father that's never there.

KENNY: But I've been going every week since I was fifteen babe.

EMILY: Do you love me?

KENNY: Yeah, I love you more than anyone I've ever met. You've saved my life you've given it meaning, you've given me something to live for, without you I'd be nothing.

EMILY: So you're gonna stop going?

KENNY: Of course not. It's all I've got to look forward to.

EMILY: What about me?

KENNY: What about you?

EMILY: See this was it. This was the test. I don't want you to stop going the football.

KENNY: What's the problem then?

EMILY: I want you to want to stop going the football.

KENNY: What?

EMILY: I want you to want to stop going the football because you love me.

KENNY: I do love you.

EMILY: You just said you wouldn't stop going the football.

KENNY: No.

EMILY: Why?

KENNY: You want me to want to stop going?

EMILY: I want you to want to want to stop going because you want me more than you want football.

KENNY: I want everything. Why can't I have both?

EMILY: Because I want you to choose me. Can you do that?

KENNY: I shouldn't have to.

EMILY: We're finished.

KENNY: Why?

EMILY: Because you don't love me.

KENNY: I do.

EMILY: You don't Ken, you love the idea of me. You love the idea that you got the girl you loved when you were in school, you love the idea of Southampton Football Club not the thing itself. You love the idea of going to the match with ya mates because it's what ya dad did and coming back to me because it's what you think you want. If you really loved me you would have said 'Yes I'll stop going'. Do you think you and all those boys with no prospects getting smashed every week are what I need in my life? And if everything's getting more expensive and you're not earning more money why should you go to the footy when you have to feed a family? Don't you think it's time you grew up and started watching on Sky? Where do I fit into this? I need someone to love me Kenny not just someone who says it.

KENNY: Southampton are never on Sky.

EMILY: You don't love me. I need a family. I'm getting older I'm not gonna look like this for ever. I need someone to love me.

KENNY: Emily I know you there's something else. What is it?

EMILY: No. I'm Rickie Lambert Kenny that's what I am. I'm fucking Rickie Lambert. And I'm gonna leave you just like he left you for Liverpool.

KENNY 482 – THE REST OF THE WORLD 9507

She leaves.

FA CUP 6th ROUND: SOUTHAMPTON VS LEEDS

KENNY 487 – THE REST OF THE WORLD 9564

They're on a coach back from Leeds.

LADS: *(Except KENNY – Singing)*

JOEY: *Who beats Leeds at Elland Road*

LADS: *We do, We do.*

COLLIN: *Who gets all the birds that we can find?*

LADS: *We do, We do.*

DAVE: *Who takes Yorkshire from behind?*

LAD: You do. You do.

It's KENNY's turn. He won't play.

JOEY: Come on mate.

KENNY: No.

JOEY: What's the matter with you mate, you look worse than that smell from the toilet.

DAVE: I don't know why we didn't just pay a bit more and get that disco van.

JOHNNO: You don't wana go to Leeds in a disco van. Can you imagine losing and driving back from Leeds in a disco van?

DAVE: Well we didn't lose did we. I would have loved a disco van.

COLLIN: We're not all made of money though are we – it's expensive as is on a coach. Yet alone a disco van.

JOEY: What's the matter with you mate? We've just beaten Leeds, we're going to Wembley.

DAVE: Who we got?

JOHNNO looks it up.

JOHNNO: Liverpool.

LAD: Oh fuck.

COLLIN: Who the fin feet got?

JOHNNO looks it up.

JOHNNO: City.

LADS: Yes!

JOEY: See we're going to Wembley and Portsmouth are gonna get mauled like dogs. What's the matter?

KENNY: I'm fine.

JOEY: Come on mate now's not the time to worry about your mum.

KENNY: It's not my mum.

COLLIN: Oh come on get over Emily she's a knob anyway she looks like a foot.

KENNY: Collin I swear to God you need to shut up or I'm going to knock you out.

COLLIN: Stop being a baby you still pissed off about the hamster?

KENNY: Course I'm still pissed off about the hamster.

COLLIN: I didn't mean to kill it.

KENNY: Yeah well I didn't mean to sleep with your sister. Maybe I'll do it again now I've broken up with Emily.

COLLIN: Look Kenny I know you're upset but there's no need to bring that up again is there.

KENNY: Why not? Easy isn't it.

COLLIN: Right. Yeah.

COLLIN lashes out at KENNY and a fight breaks out.

KENNY 487 – THE REST OF THE WORLD 9565

KENNY'S MUM'S HOUSE

MUM: Kenny

KENNY: *(To audience.)* I bet Le Tiss doesn't have to put up with this shit.

(To MUM.) What do you want mum?

MUM: Don't talk to me like that

KENNY: Sorry. What?

MUM: Come here. Don't shout.

KENNY: I spend enough time with you as it is, I can't actually need to speak to you now.

MUM: Kenny

KENNY: *(To audience.)* Today she's decided to live downstairs. In-between the sitting room and kitchen. So to talk to her I have to go all the way down and in this mood it takes four times as long.

KENNY goes downstairs. His MUM's in bed.

KENNY: You alright?

MUM: What happened to your face, you look like the Elephant man.

KENNY: Na I'm fine mum just got in a scrap in Leeds. Mad there yano Northerners.

MUM: Put some ice on it.

KENNY: I will. What do you want?

MUM: Could you hang those new knickers up for me?

KENNY 487 – THE REST OF THE WORLD 9566

KENNY: What?

MUM: I need them dry for tomorrow.

KENNY: Can't you wear some other ones? You've got a whole drawer full of them.

MUM: …Carl's coming round.

KENNY: Come on! I don't need to know that.

MUM: I'm still young I still have yano… A life.

KENNY: You can't be having more sex than me.

MUM: Well I don't know.

KENNY: What do you mean you don't know?

MUM: I don't know how much you're getting.

KENNY: Are you having sex?!

MUM: …

KENNY: Well you're beating me then aren't ya.

KENNY 487 – THE REST OF THE WORLD 9567

KENNY: Fucking hell. Fine. I'll do it.

MUM: Kenny you know I love you don't ya.

KENNY: What is it Mum?

MUM: Carl's moving in…

KENNY 487 – THE REST OF THE WORLD 9568

MUM: You can't keep looking after me forever.

KENNY: Is it what you want?

MUM: Yeah. He can look after me. You can go and do your thing. Be a grown up.

KENNY: I'm twenty-nine, I am a grownup.

MUM: I didn't mean it like that Ken.

KENNY: Alright.

MUM: I didn't.

KENNY: Alright mum. I'll sort your knickers out.

MUM: Thanks.

KENNY: Hope you're alright down here tonight.

MUM: Yeah. It'll be fine. It's cosy.

KENNY: If you need me give me a shout.

MUM: Alright. Night Ken.

KENNY: Night.

MUM: Ken?

KENNY: What?

MUM: I just want both of us to be as happy as we can be, regardless of all this. Alright? I just want us to make the best of this situation.

KENNY: Yeah. Love you Mum.

MUM: Love you. And thanks. I mean it Ken. Not many kids would have done what you've done for me.

KENNY: *(To audience.)* Three more weeks. Three weeks of getting fucked. Three weeks of being a lad. Three weeks of Southampton home loses, three weeks of Carl moving in and three weeks of not having Emily. Everything is awful. I've never felt so alone.

A SCHOOL REUNION

KENNY 487 – THE REST OF THE WORLD 9632

COMMENTATOR 1: And here we are at the school reunion. How's it looking Gabby?

COMMENTATOR 2: Yes the lads are off to London tomorrow but before then it's time to catch up with old school friends at a fancy dress shin dig.

COMMENTATOR 1: The lads have decided to go as the Brazil football team. Nice work lads. Except for this.

… JOHNNO has blacked up.

JOEY: No. Go home.

JOHNNO: What? Why?

DAVE: You can't black up you knobhead.

JOHNNO: Why not? We're the Brazil team. One of us is going to be black?

DAVE: I'm black.

JOHNNO: Yeah but there'd be more than one of us wouldn't there.

DAVE: It's racist.

JOHNNO: Why's it racist?

DAVE: I dunno it just is. Go and get washed.

JOHNNO: No.

COLLIN: Well I'm not going in with you like that.

JOHNNO: Why not? There were no black people in our year.

DAVE: I'm black!

JOHNNO: Yeah but not really.

DAVE: It's really racist!

JOHNNO: I'm not washing. It's really expensive getting all the shoe polish for this.

JOEY: You're wearing shoe polish? Are you not getting high?

JOHNNO: I feel a bit hazy yeah.

DAVE: Go and get washed.

JOHNNO: Really?

DAVE: Yes.

JOHNNO: What if I just wash my face and arms?

COLLIN: Are you wearing it all over your body?

JOHNNO: Yeah. Obviously.

JOEY: Why have ya done that?

JOHNNO: In case we took our tops off.

COLLIN: Why would we take our tops off?

JOHNNO: It's a school reunion, its fancy dress, it could get wild.

KENNY: It's not going to get wild. Wash your face and arms and just keep your top on. Come on, let's go.

They enter the party. Glitter balls and shite music. The rest of the cast are in fancy dress.

KENNY: *(To audience.)* Everyone's looking old. I'm shitting myself Emily's gonna be here. I can't speak. I decide to get pissed.

SARAH JANE walks past dressed as an ostrich.

Sarah Jane. If Emily's too good for me, maybe that's my type, maybe that's what I do now… Maybe I should fall in love with her…

Alright

SARAH JANE: Alright. You?

KENNY: Yeah good. What you up to these days?

SARAH JANE: Married an accountant.

KENNY 487 – THE REST OF THE WORLD 9633

KENNY: …… Oh nice.

SARAH JANE: You?

KENNY: … Yeah same. Well not married an accountant I'm er… I'm dating… Just want a family yano. That's what we're all after isn't it. I mean I was dating… She broke up with me because I got Matt Le Tissier's face tattooed on my arse.

SARAH JANE: OK. That's er… Yeah. Cool. Well yano… What are you doing these days?

KENNY: Cabbie mate.

SARAH JANE: Where you living?

KENNY: Me mam's still.

SARAH JANE: Right. Well. That's cool.

A Mega Tune from their youth comes on…

SARAH JANE: It's ma tune. I've got to go. Nice to catch up with you. Nice to hear your…yeah. Lovely to see you!

KENNY 487 – THE REST OF THE WORLD 9634

KENNY: Not bothered anyway you stink of quavers. *(To audience.)* Sometimes you shoot and miss but you don't always want to score.

He starts stealing some food and drink, filling his pockets and bag with it…

COMMENTATOR 1: And here he is, the fly in the soup, the oil in the water, the x in the x. Jeremy McArdle, the last thing in the world Kenny wants to see. And to make things worse… He's dressed as a sheriff.

In walks JEREMY MCARDLE. Dressed as a Sheriff. Fully clocking him.

JEREMY MCARDLE: Kenny Glynn. What are you doing?

KENNY: Oh er… Yeah. Off to London tomorrow. Long trip. Stocking up.

JEREMY MCARDLE: Good mate good. You look well, you look healthy and rested. What you been doing?

KENNY: … Ya mum.

JEREMY MCARDLE: Very good.

KENNY: Sorry. Not sure why I said that. Bit childish. What do you do?

JEREMY MCARDLE: Opened a business didn't I.

KENNY 487 – THE REST OF THE WORLD 9635

KENNY: What selling cars or something?

JEREMY MCARDLE: Nar mate. I sell dreams.

KENNY: Serious?

JEREMY MCARDLE: Yeah mate. I sell dreams and I save people. I'm like a modern day Christ.

KENNY: Right.

JEREMY MCARDLE: What are you doing?

KENNY: Me? I'm er…studying.

JEREMY MCARDLE: What you studying?

KENNY: Renewable energy.

JEREMY MCARDLE: I just bumped into gimpy Dave, isn't he doing that?

KENNY: No he's doing his A-Levels. I'm doing an Open Uni degree.

JEREMY MCARDLE: Right. Little gay. Always knew he was a bender yano – can imagine him just like putting his – in someone's – urgh.

KENNY: So what if he's gay?

JEREMY MCARDLE: I'm only kidding

KENNY: Nah man – so what if he's gay?

JEREMY MCARDLE: I'm joking man.

KENNY: Well that's not funny is it? He's one of my best mates and he's gay – why is that something you can take the piss out of?

JEREMY MCARDLE: Come on. He's gay.

KENNY: So what? What does that matter?

JEREMY MCARDLE: Sorry. So, you married?

KENNY: Girlfriend. I'm seeing Emily now.

JEREMY MCARDLE: Emily Emily?

KENNY: Yeah.

JEREMY MCARDLE: Wow. Didn't see that coming. Everyone settles. Nice bhajis.

KENNY: I mean it's not settling, it's love. It's definitely love. Yeah so. These sausage rolls are nice.

JEREMY MCARDLE: She's dynamite. We had good times. The birth mark hey. On the… Yano. When she does that… yano. Yeah. Good for you. I miss that. Wish my misses would do that but she's got too much self respect. Kids?

KENNY: No. You?

JEREMY MCARDLE: One. Boy. Titus. Arse like a fucking bull.

KENNY: Titus?

JEREMY MCARDLE: Yep. Anyway, must do the rounds, got my car parked on a single yellow line

KENNY: What you driving?

JEREMY MCARDLE: Got a reconditioned 1957 BMW 507 mate. Look like fucking JFK in it.

KENNY: Hey. Do you remember laughing when my dad died?

JEREMY MCARDLE: No mate… I wouldn't do that. We were friends in school weren't we? We sat next to each other at the last game at the Dell.

KENNY: …. Yeah mate… Yeah cool. Must have been someone else.

JEREMY MCARDLE: Yeah probably. Probably that Joey. Remember him? The one with the face like a boob? Yano, used to be sick at footy. Hurt his leg or something. Probably for the best. Bellends like that, don't want them being rich do we?

KENNY: Dunno mate. Dunno.

JEREMY MCARDLE: We're the winners Ken, you and me, and that's all that matters. At least we're winning right. At least we're winning. I'll see you later.

KENNY: Yeah… At least we're winning.

JEREMY MCARDLE: Yeah… Ciao Bella. Oh. How's ya mum?

KENNY: *(To audience.)* I hang around and have few a more awkward conversations with people I've never cared about.

I've done it wrong. Maybe we've all done it wrong –

JOHNNO tries to take his top off but is stopped by everyone else.

JOHNNO: Ladies and Gentleman. A toast to the class of 2003.

EVERYONE: Hurrah

JOHNNO: And now a song from our youth…

JOHNNO does a song, the party kicks off. Everyone throws food.

EMILY almost materialises behind KENNY.

EMILY is dressed as EMILY.

EMILY: We need to talk

KENNY: I knew there was something else.

EMILY: Can we go outside?

KENNY: … Alright. If we have to.

They go outside.

EMILY: It's cold.

KENNY: Yeah.

EMILY: Listen. I don't want to freak you out. I'm pregnant.

KENNY 487 – THE REST OF THE WORLD 9636

KENNY: Is it mine?

EMILY: Of course it's yours Ken.

KENNY: Right.

EMILY: But it doesn't change anything. Everything I said I mean I just… I wanted to tell you at brunch but I couldn't. It was just… I'm sorry.

KENNY gets his phone out.

EMILY: What are you doing?

KENNY: Cancelling London.

EMILY: You were going to London?

KENNY: Tomorrow.

EMILY: Why?

KENNY: Semis. FA Cup.

EMILY: Why are you cancelling it?

KENNY: Doesn't matter does it? What do you need from me?

EMILY: I dunno. I dunno what to do.

KENNY: … Right. And I'm not just saying this because I'm pissed right. But listen. Let's move in together. I'm not having a child grow up in their grandparents' house. If I'm going to spend money on this shit at the very least I'm leaving Mum's. She's got Carl living there so she doesn't need me. As long as we're close. We can put some cash down and rent a little flat or something. Get the baby everything it wants, everything it needs.

EMILY: You can't afford that.

KENNY: I'll do double hours in the cab.

EMILY: I don't believe ya.

KENNY: I'll prove it then,

EMILY: OK.

KENNY: And let's get married. This is gonna be the best thing that's ever happen to us Emily.

EMILY: This is exactly what I mean.

KENNY: What?

EMILY: You don't mean it.

KENNY: I love you.

EMILY: You're just saying this because I'm pregnant.

KENNY: Na I do.

EMILY: Right OK. Look I'm going. I'll wait to hear from you about everything.

KENNY: I do love you.

EMILY: OK.

KENNY: Emily

EMILY: What?

KENNY: I do. Shall I come home with ya?

EMILY: Go home and see ya mum

EMILY leaves.

KENNY 487 – THE REST OF THE WORLD 9637

He goes home.

COMMENTATOR 1: And that's it for Kenny Glynn

COMMENTATOR 2: He's calling it a night.

COMMENTATOR 1: God knows how he gets home.

INSIDE THE HOUSE

His MUM is trying to climb the stairs.

KENNY 487 – THE REST OF THE WORLD 9638

KENNY: What are you doing mum?

MUM: Nothing.

KENNY: Are you trying to get upstairs?

MUM: Leave me alone I'll be fine.

KENNY: Let me help mum.

MUM: Just leave me alone!

KENNY walks into the kitchen and, from a distance, watches her scramble up the stairs. It's heartbreaking.

KENNY: What's going on?

CARL: She knows she's not going to be able to walk. She just wants to get upstairs.

KENNY starts crying.

CARL: I know you're emotional.

KENNY: My ex is pregnant and now this in one night. Yeah I'm emotional.

Something inside him snaps and he smashes something up.

CARL: Have you told your mum?

KENNY: I don't wana talk about that. I'll sort that out. It's nothing to do with you. What are we gonna do about mum?

CARL: Right. Well. What we need to do is simple actually. She's alright in general, she hates it down there, it's just getting up those stairs if she could do then she'd be pretty much independent if we keep doing little things for her so I think what we need to do, and I know this is grim Ken but it's my field and it's the right thing to do, what we need to do is get a stair lift. I know it'll look weird but that's what we need to do. They cost £3,000.

KENNY 487 – THE REST OF THE WORLD 9639

KENNY: I just can't do it Carl.

CARL: I know it's a lot but I've thought about it and I didn't think I could ask you for that so what I thought I'd do is, I'll get a loan and you can pay me back, when you can.

KENNY: Right.

CARL: You don't have to if you can't afford it.

KENNY: I can support my own mum.

CARL: Right. So what do we do?

KENNY: I'll pay half now. I can get you the £1,500

CARL: You sure?

KENNY: Yeah I'm sure.

KENNY 487 – THE REST OF THE WORLD 9640

CARL: Right. I'll sort it out then.

KENNY: Yeah. OK.

CARL goes to help MUM get up the stairs.

KENNY: Right.

WONGA

A man comes in to serve KENNY… It's JEREMY MCARDLE.

KENNY 487 – THE REST OF THE WORLD 9641

KENNY: Right.

JEREMY MCARDLE: Right.

KENNY: Jeremy McArdle.

JEREMY MCARDLE: Kenny G – Ah. Hi. How's ya mum?

KENNY: How is this you selling dreams?

JEREMY MCARDLE: Well. You know how Christ used to have a temple where all the fucking poor and needy and that used to come? And he used to like… Perform miracles and make all their problems go away. Well this is that isn't it. Exactly the same. People come in here with problems and I lend them some money and then they leave and their problems go away.

KENNY: But they owe you money.

JEREMY MCARDLE: Well yeah but better me than the gas or electric company, they can cut you off. Anyway. What can I do for you?

KENNY: I need some money.

JEREMY MCARDLE: OK. How much?

KENNY: £5,000.

JEREMY MCARDLE: Are you in trouble?

KENNY: It's good being a winner isn't it.

SOUTHAMPTON VS LIVERPOOL.
FA CUP SEMI-FINAL

KENNY, MUM and CARL after watching Southampton Vs Liverpool on Sky.

MUM: He's good that Schiderlin isn't he Ken?

KENNY: Yes Mum.

MUM: I like Fonte's hair he looks like a little pony.

KENNY: Yes Mum.

MUM: I still can't believe you're not there. How come you haven't gone?

KENNY: Didn't feel like.

CARL: Oh look at this Clyne is… Oh my God. Did you see that? Did you see that Ken? We're beating Liverpool. I bet Lambert is gutted now.

MUM: Was that Lovren's fault?

CARL: Yeah.

MUM: We don't like him do we.

CARL: No.

MUM: We don't like him do we Ken?

KENNY: No we don't Mum.

CARL: Lallana is wasted on them. Henderson and Gerrard won't let him do anything. He's awful. What's he doing there? What's he doing? What's he doing? What on earth is he doing?

KENNY: Shut up.

Peep. Peep. Peep.

Wembley is swarming with Southampton fans singing.

MUM: You not pleased Ken?

KENNY: Yeah I'm buzzing.

MUM: Ken.

KENNY: What?

MUM: I'll buy you a ticket. Remember I always said? I always said that if Southampton go to the FA cup final I'll buy you a ticket.

KENNY: Yeah. You did.

MUM: Right what's the matter with you then? I'm not having you behaving like this.

KENNY: I've got Emily pregnant and we've broken up. She won't talk to me.

MUM: Was it planned?

KENNY: What do you think?

MUM: I'll put the tea on.

She leaves.

KENNY: *(To audience.)* There is nothing worse than your parents being disappointed. I'd rather they were angry.

KENNY 487 – THE REST OF THE WORLD 9642

CARL: Let her pay for the ticket Ken.

KENNY: I'm not going.

CARL: You have to.

KENNY: Why?

CARL: Do you know what's amazing about when we won it in 1976?

KENNY: No.

CARL: We were shit and we still won it. And do you know what was amazing about it?

KENNY: What?

CARL: Because that day I realised that anyone can win the FA cup if they deserve it. You've been slaving your whole life, looking after your mum, following a team that haven't given back what you've given to them, and you're about to be a father. You deserve a day out. I'll stay with her on the day. I've seen it. Even the teams that don't think they deserve it deserve a trip to Wembley when they work as hard as you.

He leaves.

GRANDSTAND VOICE: And the results are in – Southampton have their match for the FA Cup Final. And, oh my god what a scorcher, it's PORTSMOUTH.

INSIDE KENNY'S BEDROOM

COMMENTATOR 2: Oh no. He's not doing this again is he.

COMMENTATOR 1: Oh this is too sad I… I just can't watch.

KENNY is in his fairy costume again.

KENNY: Show yourself.

… No one comes.

KENNY 487 – THE REST OF THE WORLD 9643

Life turns up and the game is the most one-sided we've ever seen it. Life is hammering him and in the middle of it…

OUTSIDE A FLAT

EMILY: What are you doing?

KENNY: This is where we're gonna live. Look listen, listen – I know it's not what you want but I'm not having a child grow up in its grandma's house right. OK? Now I've rented this place and you can live in it alone or live in it with me but I'm trying to give that child a home. I'll pay for it. It's on me.

EMILY: Where did you get the money from?

KENNY: I've saved up and I got a deposit.

EMILY: Why?

KENNY: Because it's the right thing to do. I'm taking responsibility OK. I'm taking it. I want to be there for that child so I've got us a house and if you don't want me in it that's fine too. I just want what's right for that child.

EMILY: OK.

KENNY: Right. So here we are.

EMILY: What do you expect me to say?

KENNY: I just want a chance to make things right. I want the best circumstances for that baby to enter the world in. I want it to have every chance it can. I want it to be in a proper family. Marry me.

EMILY: Why?

KENNY: If you don't marry me for me, marry me for this. I know what it's like not having a dad and I wouldn't wish it on anyone. I want it to have everything; I think it's the right thing to do even if it's not perfect. Will you marry me?

EMILY: Alright yeah OK.

KENNY 487 – THE REST OF THE WORLD 9644

KENNY: Leave it with me, I'll sort everything out, I don't want you to do anything.

EMILY: Alright.

KENNY: Thought it would be better than this.

EMILY: Me too. Right I'm off then.

KENNY: Emily?

EMILY: What?

KENNY: Take the keys. It's yours now. I'll pay for it as long as you need it.

EMILY: Alright.

KENNY: Emily?

EMILY: What?

KENNY: Do you want me to move in?

EMILY: I dunno Ken. I'll see you later.

KENNY 487 – THE REST OF THE WORLD 9645

Life goes mental and scores some more.

Grandstand Voice Millbrook Saints Vs Ashurt

Peep.

Grandstand Voice Millbrook Saints 3 Ashurt 9.

FA CUP FINAL: SOUTHAMPTON VS PORTSMOUTH.

COMMENTATOR 1: And looks at this what a colourful assortment of people here to take Kenny Glynn on his stag. But oh no what's this? He hasn't got a costume. He's like Luis Suarez in an actual fight – horribly out of place.

JOEY: Where's ya fancy dress?

KENNY: I dunno Joe.

JOEY: Come on it's ya stag. Where's ya costume?

KENNY: I haven't got one. I thought you lads were getting me one. It's my stag.

JOEY: Well we haven't got ya one.

MUM: Don't worry, you've got that one in ya bedroom. The one you always wear.

KENNY: What you talking about?

MUM: You know the –

KENNY: Right. Come on lads.

JOEY: Na wait. You can't go without a costume.

They go outside.

MUM: Bye love. Have a nice stag. Don't drink too much.

KENNY: I won't mum.

MUM: Don't want you getting lost in London and falling in the Thames.

KENNY: Won't mum, I'm twenty-nine.

MUM: You can still drown. A boy in my class from school went on a stag once.

KENNY: What happened?

MUM: He died.

KENNY: Right. Very good. Bye mum. I've got my mobile on. Oh shit wait there.

His goes upstairs to get his dad's scarf and comes down again. The lads are getting in the Limo.

… When they're in the lads reveal the costume for KENNY… And it's ridiculous.

KENNY 487 – THE REST OF THE WORLD 9646

INSIDE THE LIMO

COMMENTATOR 2: Who'd have thought it the Millbrook Saints on the way to London

COMMENTATOR 1: And here we are picking up in the middle of the best man's speech.

JOEY: As best man it's my job to lay down the rules of the stag: The first rule is, as ever in a court of ladness, be a fucking lad and the second and most important rule is…. Never get deep. There will be no getting deep. Can I get an Amen.

LADS: AMEN.

JOEY: Can I get a hallelujah?

LADS: Hallelujah.

JOEY: Can I get a PRAISE THE LORD!

LADS: PRAISE THE LORD!!!

There's a beeping from another car. They pull next to JEREMY MCARDLE. KENNY pisses into a can and pours it on the windscreen.

KENNY: TAKE THAT YA BELLEND. WAHAY.

KENNY 488 – THE REST OF THE WORLD 9646

This is so good. I'm tired as fuck but it doesn't matter BECAUSE WE'RE GOING OUT. THIS IS THE MOMENT WE'VE BEEN WAITING FOR ALL OUR LIVES.

LADS: WAHAY

JOEY: You excited Ken?

KENNY: What's it like?

DAVE: I dunno am not married am I.

KENNY: Not the wedding. Wembley.

DAVE: Magic mate. It's magic. It's like stepping into happiness.

KENNY: Sounds good to me mate. Sounds good to me. Pass us that tin.

A STRIP CLUB

COMMENTATOR 1: A Strip Club. There's lots of naked ladies about and I am getting uncomfortable.

COMMENTATOR 2: Anyone with young children might want to cover their eyes at this point.

COLLIN: This place is horrible.

JOEY: OK guys it's speech time.

DAVE: Again?

JOEY: We've been through a hell of a lot right and I just want to say this –

DAVE: I thought we said no getting deep. Shut up man and eat your calamari.

KENNY: Bit weird eating squid in a strip club.

JOHNNO: It's what the locals do.

KENNY: Really?

DAVE: I don't think this is what the locals do.

JOHNNO: It's what the locals do.

KENNY: Really?

DAVE: I don't think this is what the locals do.

JOHNNO: Well it must be mustn't it. Or it wouldn't be on the menu… And that's what we're doing for your stag. Being local Londoners.

KENNY: You getting a dance?

JOEY: I reckon so. Why not.

KENNY: Really?

JOEY: Yeah why not?

KENNY: I mean is that OK? Is that something we do? Do we get strippers?

JOHNNO: Today we do mate. Today we're not ourselves are we. And it's your stag. We can be as wild as like. Here you go.

KENNY: What is it?

JOHNNO: Lad card. License to be a lad.

KENNY: How much for a dance?

JOHNNO: On me mate. Happy stag.

COLLIN: Let's go.

They are led to two booths facing each other.

KENNY: Oh pack it in.

KENNY 488 – THE REST OF THE WORLD 9647

Not you. Him. He's putting me off. He's rubbing his thighs.

COLLIN: Stop looking at me ya tit you'll ruin this for me.

KENNY: Can you like, turn around or something.

COLLIN: Shut up.

KENNY: You're putting me off.

COLLIN: No.

KENNY: Jesus.

A beat.

That's it?

We gave you like £20

Well… How much has Zorro given?

COLLIN: I'm not Zoro. £200.

KENNY: I heard her. How long's he gonna be?

COLLIN: A while.

KENNY: Jesus

COLLIN: I'm in the lone ranger.

KENNY slumps out. There's only JOEY left.

KENNY: Where's everyone gone?

JOEY: Getting dances.

KENNY: You alright mate?

JOEY: Could have been me today mate.

KENNY: I know yeah

JOEY: I could have been playing. Could have been leading them out.

KENNY: I know yeah. Cheer up.

JOEY: I hate it when people say 'cheer up'. My life's a failure. I work on sites. I'm fat. I'm bald. I'm single. I'm a mess. I messed up the one chance I had at doing something important.

KENNY: Mate. It wasn't your fault. Look at me. I'm marrying a woman who doesn't really want to marry me. Live with my mum and drive cabs. We're the majority. There's more people like us than there are like Adam Lallana.

JOEY: Do you think if there wasn't football there'd be a revolution? How many people stand at St Mary's every week that are raging with life and letting it all out on a Saturday.

KENNY: Thousands. If it wasn't coming out at football matches it would come out in fists and blood.

JOEY: How did it get so shit?

KENNY: Mate. People look up to you. Every time you walk into a room you lift up everyone around you after what you've been through and still be the soul of the party, I couldn't do it. Let's just enjoy ourselves. It's my stag. And when we win today it's gonna be the best we've ever felt in our lives – teams like us don't come this far and lose mate. It's our time, we've waited so long for this and today it's all so gonna pay out. It has to pay out. Because if it doesn't what are bothering for. So let's do the only thing we can do mate. Let's enjoy it. Yeah? Yeah? Yeah? Come on. Yeah? Yeah? Yeaah… Yeah? Yeah? Yeah? Yeah? Yeah?

JOEY: Yeah

KENNY: YEAH!?

JOEY: YEAH!

KENNY: YEAHHHH! Let's go

JOEY: Can't believe I didn't like you in primary school. You're the best mate I could ever have.

KENNY: Hey. No. Getting. Deep. We agreed that. Yeah? Yeah? No getting deep. Never get deep. Never ever get deep.

JOEY: YOU'RE RIGHT. LET'S GO!

KENNY 489 – THE REST OF THE WORLD 9647

COMMENTATOR 2: Off they go into London.

A BOOKIES

COMMENTATOR 1: Treading a fine line is Ken here.

COMMENTATOR 2: 5k in debt and going up and he's in a bookies – dangerous game.

COLLIN: £3 on 2-0. £1 on Rodregus first scorer and £1 on 0-3.

JOHNNO: You're betting on us losing 3-0?

COLLIN: Yeah.

DAVE: Fuck that. £4 we win 3-0.

JOEY: £6 2-0

KENNY: £100 1-0 Taric first scorer.

JOEY: You sure mate?

KENNY: Yeah mate. I'm gonna have a fucking good time today. Go big or go home. In fact. £300. 1-0 Tadic first scorer.

LADS: Shiiiit!

DAVE: Can you afford that, mate?

JOEY: Shut up, Dave.

COLLIN: £30 on 0-0 after ninety and Portsmouth wins on penalties. Danny East scores the winning penalty.

KENNY: As if. Stop being so pessimistic, it's my stag.

COLLIN: I'm not here for your stag Kenny. I'm here for the football.

KENNY: Fine.

OUTSIDE WEMBLEY

They lose themselves in a swarm of other fans, a sea of red and white.

COMMENTATOR 1: And here we at Wembley, a sea of red and white

COMMENTATOR 2: And blue and white as well.

COMMENTATOR 2: And looks who's followed us all the way to London…

A FANATIC: Hey! This is the holiest moment of our lives, today we touch Heaven. There is a story of a man eating dinner. He has the same dinner every week, every night and one day he looks up at his family and he goes – 'I'm happy' and he asks his wife why and she says it's because tonight, tonight Toby, God is here. *(To KENNY.)* I'm looking at you – you're about to find God in here, on the pitch, in the stands, on the grass, this is a holy day for you. For all of us. This is how we touch Heaven. By being here. Being God for The Saints. We make this holy. YEAHHHHHHH!!!!

FANS: Yeahhhhh!!!

THE FANATIC is carried away by the fans.

KENNY: *(To audience.)* In this moment we're part of something bigger. Like being baptised into this swarm of noise.

Oh when The Saints, go marching in…

INSIDE WEMBLEY

The songs around them are deafening.

KENNY: This is why the FA Cup is the greatest competition on earth. This is the moment that I've been waiting for my whole life. This is the FA CUP FINAL.

From this scene all we hear is the sound of the football match.

KENNY gets lost in the noise.

He scores a couple of goals against life.

KENNY's DAD appears on the pitch.

KENNY goes to him.

KENNY: Dad. I've got the scarf dad. Just like you asked.

KENNY 490 – THE REST OF THE WORLD 9647

He puts it round his DAD's neck. Back to the noise of the game.

Lots of cheering.

Someone is scoring!!!

Someone is winning!!!

THE LIMO

The silence is palpable.

JOEY: I'm not going again.

JOHNNO: Na me neither.

DAVE: It's just a game.

JOEY: It's quite clearly not just a game or we wouldn't be this upset about it would we.

DAVE: Alright mate.

JOHNNO: I think there's something quite comforting about it. Yeah we just lost the FA cup final but the league starts again in a few weeks. Quite comforting that isn't it. Like a clean slate.

JOEY: What's the point in getting to the final if you don't even win.

COLLIN: I don't care I'm minted. 5k.

KENNY: Great nice one. For betting against The Saints.

COLLIN: No need to be an arsehole about it.

KENNY: I don't see what else I can be about it.

COLLIN: Why? Coz you're in debt?

DAVE: Careful Collin

KENNY: How did you even know?

COLLIN: Jeremy McArdle was saying in Ninety Degrees

KENNY: I bet you were pissing yourself weren't ya.

COLLIN: Of course not.

JOEY: Carl said something too.

KENNY: Great. You fucking love this don't you?

COLLIN: You're a dick.

KENNY: You're a dick.

JOEY: Do it Collin.

JOHNNO: Do it.

KENNY: Do what?

DAVE: Do it Collin.

COLLIN: Take it.

He holds out the envelope.

KENNY: Don't take the piss out of me

DAVE: He's not.

COLLIN: Take it. I haven't got a family. You have. All I've got to do is get drunk on a Saturday. You need this more than me.

KENNY: I'm not taking your charity.

COLLIN: It's not charity. I want it back.

KENNY: I don't want it.

JOEY: Take it.

COLLIN: Take it.

KENNY: No.

COLLIN: Just get over the fact I'm a dickhead and take it.

KENNY 491 – THE REST OF THE WORLD 9647

KENNY: OK. I'll pay you back.

COLLIN: I know you will.

They look at each other.

COLLIN: Sorry about the hamster.

KENNY: You're such a dick.

KENNY puts his hand out. COLLIN shakes it.

COLLIN hands over an envelope of cash.

KENNY: Thank you

JOEY takes the envelope from KENNY.

JOEY: We'll sort this out for yer.

JEREMY'S HOUSE

The LADS (but not KENNY) go to JEREMY's house.

COMMENTATOR 1: And this is interesting the boys have gone their separate ways to settle scores for Kenny. This could go terribly, if they play it wrong they could end up getting arrested.

JOEY: Jeremy McArdle. This town ain't big enough for the two of us.

JEREMY MCARDLE: What can I do for you Spiderman?

JOEY: I think you're a piece of shit Jeremy.

JEREMY MCARDLE: Is that you Joey?

JOEY: Maybe maybe not.

JEREMY MCARDLE: You threw wee on my car

JOEY: … no.

JEREMY MCARDLE: … Are you here to beat me up?

JOEY: No Jeremy I'm just here to tell you we think you're horrible – you are rinsing the desperate. That's one thing I won't allow here. How do you sleep at night?

JEREMY MCARDLE: On a bed of money. See yer Spidey!!

JOEY: No. I'd love to beat the shit out of you but what would that prove?

JEREMY: I'll call the police

JOEY: Just put this money in the Kenny Glynn account. And if it's not clear on Monday I'll be back and every time I hear you've been lending money to people you know can't pay it back we'll be here. You get me?

JEREMY MCARDLE: Joey – Is this blackmail?

JOEY: No mate what you're doing is blackmail. And I might be Joey, I might not be. Put that money in and clear that account.

JEREMY MCARDLE: If that makes you feel like a superhero – you idiot. You failure. You has-been.

KENNY 492 – THE REST OF THE WORLD 9647

JOEY: Whatever.

JEREMY MCARDLE: Laters gays.

DAVE takes off his mask/ costume/ thing covering his face.

JEREMY MCARDLE: I knew it was you!

DAVE: Yeah it's me. I'm gay and what? I like men. I like men. I like them alright? So what? It's not an insult, it just makes you look like an arsehole. It's just something I am. You wouldn't say laters black. Or laters jew would you? No.

JEREMY: McArlde Come on, it's gays. Gays are funny.

DAVE nuts him.

DAVE: I feel sorry for you.

JEREMY: Why?

DAVE: You just got knocked down by a gay.

Pay off that debt.

He puts his hat back on.

They leave. The lads walk the entire span of the theatre. They're making a very long journey. And it should feel like they're travelling to the north pole and they're never out of sight of the audience.

COMMENTATOR 1: Errrr… Nice one boys. I think. Where's Kenny Glynn?

EMILY'S HOUSE

EMILY: What?

KENNY: I need to talk to ya.

EMILY: Go on then.

KENNY: I know you think I'm pissed.

EMILY: You are.

KENNY: I wana talk to ya.

EMILY: What have you got to say?

KENNY: Look. All I'm gonna say is this. Today we lost the FA Cup Final and tonight I travelled back in a limousine with my mates. I should have been heartbroken but I wasn't because they were there – those lads. They've sorted me out, Emily. They've looked out for me. They paid for my mum's stair lift. They did it. Someone told me life was about teamwork, about working for other people so they work for you and I'd forgotten that. And with you… I took you for granted – I got the fit bird I wanted – and I thought that was enough.

We lost the FA Cup Final – but I didn't give a shit coz I knew I had a chance to come back to you. To you. To you. My whole life I've been scared of wanting you, of talking to you, of thinking about you because deep down I didn't think I'd ever get you. But now you're here, now we're this close I'm not letting you go. You are the only thing I've ever really wanted, forget football, forget the FA cup, forget Millbrook it's you.

And I promise you now – I want to do for that baby and for you what my mates've done for me. I want to be the best person I can be. You are the only reason I get out of bed in the morning because without you it's just me getting pissed and watching football and I'll do anything to have the right to work to make this work. I'm just asking for a chance to prove that I'm the one person on this planet that is going to give you everything.

The LADS appear.

EMILY: Is this about to get weird Ken?

KENNY: I dunno – it's a gamble. My last penalty.

He turns to the LADS.

Now!

The LADS start singing EMILY's song.

I took you for granted.

I'm sorry

I've always loved you, even when you turned me down
I loved you and when you said 'yes' and didn't mean it I
loved you.

Emily?

EMILY: What?

He gets on one knee.

KENNY: Will you marry me?

She pulls him back to his feet.

EMILY: It's worth a try isn't it.

KENNY: I love you.

EMILY: I've never believed you before.

KENNY: Emily – thank you.

EMILY: I'll see you tomorrow.

KENNY 493 – THE REST OF THE WORLD 9647

KENNY: Is that a promise?

EMILY: That's a promise.

KENNY: That's all I wanted to hear. I'm gonna go before you
change your mind. Goodbye. Oh and before I forget.

EMILY: What?

KENNY: You look beautiful tonight.

He leaves.

JOHNNO: Right, lads – big day tomorrow.

KENNY: Yes mate.

JOHNNO: Last ever game of the Millbrook Saints!!

LADS: Yeahhhh!!

DAVE: And then a wedding or something.

LADS: YEAH! Lads lads lads lads lads.

COMMENTATOR 1: Millbrook Saints Vs. West End Warriors

They LADS get ready for the wedding – at the same time they play for Millbrook… It's goal heavy. 3-3. Last second pen falls to… KENNY GLYNN. He scores. They win.

KENNY 494 – THE REST OF THE WORLD 9647

LADS: WAHAY!

THE WEDDING

Everyone in suits and dresses.

EMILY comes down the aisle.

They stand opposite each other.

KENNY holds a ring near the end of EMILY's finger.

KENNY: Will you give me the chance to make you happy?

EMILY: Yeah.

KEN: Yeah?

EMILY: Yeah.

KEN: Yeah?

EMILY: YEAH

They kiss.

KENNY 495 – THE REST OF THE WORLD 9648

Cheers.

There is lots of red and white confetti.

KENNY 496 – THE REST OF THE WORLD 9648

Music plays.

They dance.

KENNY 497 – THE REST OF THE WORLD 9648

EMILY: You don't have to stop going to the match you know.

KENNY: Really?

EMILY: Yeah. Just don't get too drunk.

KENNY: I don't feel like it'll bother me now.

EMILY: Why?

KENNY: When you're a kid you want to be a footballer, and then you become a fan and you hope that you'll win something and then the day comes and you realise it's just series of moments, it's those moments that are important, making them alive and not just in football in everything. And it's those moments, Le Tissier scoring the last goal at the Dell, Joey getting injured, Adkins getting us to the premiership, seeing how brave my Mum is, going to Wembley, standing here with you, having that baby… It's these moments that are life. That's what's important.

He kisses her. The scoreboard changes to –

KENNY AND EMILY VS. THE REST OF THE WORLD. 0-0.

COMMENTATOR 1: And it looks like our time is over. Time for one last trip home.

HOME

MUM uses the stair-lift and gets upstairs. Her and CARL dance.

KENNY & EMILY 1 – THE REST OF THE WORLD 0

ON THE STREETS OF SOUTHAMPTON

(But still in the theatre.)

A FANATIC: I know no one listens to me! But….listen because there's no one here to stop me. Ok… we'll always worship, learn lessons, and no matter what's new – whether it's new stadiums, new players, new fans, some things are constant. This city will always be here. This club will always be here. Side by side in this city, in these colours, on these streets. We search for a moment.

And we keep looking. And we will keep looking together. Our children. And their children. And their children will hunt together forever. In the red and white of this club.

The New Junior Millbrook Saints Team line up. All kids. KENNY and the old boys watch.

GRANDSTAND VOICE: Millbrook Saints Juniors Vs. Totton JSC

Peep.

GRANDSTAND VOICE: Millbrook Saints 17 Totton Juniors 2

Peep. Peep. Peep.

BY THE SAME AUTHOR

Chapel Street
9781849434263

Bottleneck
9781849434379

Eisteddfod
9781849433860

Beats North
With Ishy Din
9781783191710

WWW.OBERONBOOKS.COM

Follow us on www.twitter.com/@oberonbooks
& www.facebook.com/oberonbook